JAPAN'S HIDDEN APARTHI

MW01142209

Japan's Hidden Apartheid

The Korean Minority and the Japanese

GEORGE HICKS

Ashgate

Aldershot • Brookfield USA • Singapore • Sydney

Published by
Ashgate Publishing Limited
Gower House
Croft Road
Aldershot
Hants GU11 3HR
England

Ashgate Publishing Company
Old Post Road
Brookfield
Vermont 05036
USA

British Library Cataloguing in Publication Data

Hicks, George
    Japan's hidden apartheid : the Korean minority and the
    Japanese
    1. Koreans - Japan - Social conditions 2. Racism - Japan
    3. Japan - Race relations
    I. Title
    305.8 ' 957 ' 052

Library of Congress Catalog Card Number: 97-73463

ISBN 1 84014 168 9

Printed and bound by Athenaeum Press, Ltd.,
Gateshead, Tyne & Wear.

Contents

Preface

Japan's Hidden Apartheid: The Korean Minority and the Japanese tells the story of Japan's Korean minority and its troubled relationship with Japanese state and society since World War II.

The story of Japan's largest minority casts important light on the nature of Japanese state and society in general and minority relations in particular. This includes the changing parameters of Japanese state policy toward Asian peoples, social tension and conflict, and approaches by minority groups to assimilation and cultural preservation.

Hundreds of thousands of Koreans were brought to Japan in the 1930s and 1940s, during Japan's colonial rule, many of them as semi-slave forced labor in mines and factories. They were the forebears of the 700,000 strong Korean minority in contemporary Japan, many of them in the second, third, or even fourth generation without Japanese citizenship and facing issues of discrimination and second class status.

A legacy of the Korean War has been the deep divisions within the Korean community in Japan, divided among groups aligned with North and South or independent of both. These divisions have shaped the responses of Koreans in Japan to issues of discrimination (such as the fingerprinting of aliens) and assimilation (Soren, the pro-North Korean group maintaining its own autonomous school system from nursery school to university).

In recent decades, as a result of the movements among Koreans, Japan's changing relationship to Asian nations, and her response to international human rights campaigns and other factors, the position of Koreans in Japan has undergone important changes: it became possible for many Koreans to become Japanese citizens; compulsory fingerprinting and other indignities have been eliminated; the Soren Korean community and its schools have entered a period of crisis with the death of Kim Il-Sung and with pressures from its members to acquire a Japanese education; Koreans in Japan spearheaded the movement to expose imperial Japan's sexual slavery of the comfort women.

vii

This volume documents far reaching legal and social changes as well as the continued legacies of discrimination in such areas as employment, education, and welfare that face the Korean minority. Koreans, who had Japanese citizenship under colonial rule, were deprived of that citizenship and the most minimal welfare benefits following World War II regardless of individual wishes. Partial improvement in their situation began with the Japan-ROK Normalization Treaty of 1965 and continued with Japan's 1979 ratification of the International Covenant on Human Rights which led to access to public housing and some local public employment; ratification in 1981 of the Treaty on the Status of Refugees brought standard welfare benefits including the national pension; in 1984 ratification of the Covenant on the Elimination of All Forms of Discrimination Against Women allowed nationality to be acquired through either parent. A 1991 agreement with the ROK led to relaxed and uniform permanent residence for all resident aliens, the end of fingerprinting, and appointment to regular teaching and some local government posts. Particular attention is paid to the intensely personal and symbolic issue of the legal status and use of Korean names against a background of forced adoption of Japanese names.

Issues of discrimination and assimilation are further explored in relation to the study of marriage patterns where mixed marriages have been the majority since the 1970s. Against these patterns of gains for the Korean minority, however, stand periodic outbursts of violence against Koreans and continued legacies of discrimination.

Many of the issues are given a human face through the experience, observations, and research of Korean activists. One of these is Yumi Lee, whose lengthy memoir on her own and her community's experience constitutes one important foundation of the research for this book. Other contemporary Korean activists are also quoted.

Korean and Japanese names are as written in East Asia: the family names first followed by the given names. Yumi Lee however is an exception. Korean names are in principle romanised according to the McCune-Reischauer system but chaotic popular usage makes departures unavoidable.

Part One
OVERVIEW

1 Japan's hidden minorities

Japan proclaims itself a homogeneous society of a unique and distinctive character. To the world at large, it is widely perceived as such. The Japanese establishment regards homogeneity as an essential element in its national ethos and power structure. It is credited as the key to Japan's outstanding success in overall development among non-Western countries, ever since its opening to the world in the mid-nineteenth century. This claimed homogeneity is also said to explain Japan's avoidance of the revolutions and other major convulsions which have affected all other major powers during the last few centuries.

It is true that by the standards of most large countries, Japan is relatively homogeneous. Nevertheless, out of a total population of 125 million about six million or over 6 percent of the population are minorities. According to the *Kodansha Encyclopedia of Japan* there are 'about three million Burakumin a caste of "untouchables" known pejoratively as the Eta ['those full of filth'] living in about 6,000 communities.' Koreans, including those who have become naturalized (about 160,000), are close to 800,000 in number. Okinawans number a million plus. Foreign workers from Asian countries other than Korea make up another million or more.

Official Japan has, in the past, denied the existence of these minorities. As a signatory to the United Nations International Covenant on Civil and Political Rights, Japan has to submit reports to the United Nations with respect to the Covenant's enforcement. The first report of 1980 stated flatly that 'minorities did not exist in Japan.' The Ainu, indigenous people of Hokkaido, and other minorities strongly protested the report. As a result, when Japan submitted its second report in 1987, it stated 'that although minorities did exist, there were no minority problems.'

Official Japan was forced to concede the existence of minorities when Prime Minister Nakasone in September 1986 claimed that Japan had a high intellectual level because it had no minorities. He drew a comparison with the United States: 'The level of knowledge in the United States is lower than in

Japan due to the considerable number of blacks, Puerto Ricans, and Mexicans.' The Japanese press hardly bothered to report this statement, but when an uproar of protest arose from the United States, Nakasone subsequently clarified his remarks. He stated that he had been misquoted and had only meant to point out that America had many remarkable scientific achievements to its credit 'despite the existence of so many troublesome minorities.'

Given this perceived importance of homogeneity, the existence of alien elements which do not fit the prevailing pattern of the larger population are felt by the authorities to present an anomalous irritant. Significant minorities exist in Japan. With the enormous recent growth of the guest worker phenomenon the minority population is in fact rising rapidly.

George A. De Vos, the leading authority in the United States on Japan's minorities, feels that the Japanese strategy of coping with the existence of problems posed by the minorities 'is avoidance or *direct denial that any such group continues to exist*, or that there is any real problem' (italics in the original).

To be Japanese is almost a definition of racial purity. A Korean Japanese would be a contradiction in terms, since a person can be either one or the other, but not both. The unavoidable contacts that do occur between people involve tension, disdain, and discrimination. Effectively, Japan practices a type of apartheid, but unlike the former policies of South Africa, it is apartheid by default rather than plan. It is also almost invisible, not only to the outside world but also to most Japanese themselves.

Who are Japan's minorities? In order of historical origin, the first are the Burakumin or 'ghetto dwellers.' These people are traditionally associated with unclean occupations, mainly involved with animal products. Their existence is a residue of premodern feudalism, though any legal discrimination was abolished along with the sweeping abolition of feudal structures in the 1870s. Movements for their emancipation from social barriers have occurred, both from within the community and from progressive administrative agencies, but much remains to be done.

The next group are the native inhabitants of the Ryukyu Islands, centered on Okinawa. The Ryukyuans are essentially ethnic Japanese but are distinguished by their long history as a maritime state. Their dialect may be related to Japanese but is unintelligible to speakers of the Japanese homeland dialects. Physically they have some affinity with Malays or Taiwanese indigenes. The majority Japanese tend to regard them as alien, even to the extent that during the post-war Allied occupation the Japanese government was prepared to relinquish territorial claim to the Ryukyus permanently in exchange for an early peace treaty.

Next are the Ainu, indigenous people of Hokkaido, with some immigrants from Southern Sakhalin, from the time of Japanese colonialism there. Along with the Ryukyuans, the Ainu were incorporated into the Japanese state during

4

its consolidation following the abolition of feudalism, when borders were defined against China in the south and imperial Russia in the north. The Ainu are ethnically quite distinct from the Japanese, marked physically by paler skin and Caucasoid build. Japanese commentators describe them as hairier than other East Asian races, though the Ainu resent this as a stereotype. Their language is equally distinct, though perhaps remotely linked to the same North Asian Altaic group as Japanese and Korean. Culturally they had not developed past the tribal stage before the intensive Japanese settlement of Hokkaido, though in recent times the Ainu Association of Hokkaido has become politically active, stimulated by the new eloquence of indigenous peoples throughout the world.

The Ainu have advocated revision of the 1899 Law on the Protection of Former Indigenes of Hokkaido and protested to the United Nations Human Rights Commission about Prime Minister Nakasone's 1986 statement that Japan 'had a uniformly high level of intelligence because it had no minorities.' This led to Japan's first admission, in its next report under the International Covenant on Civil and Political Rights, that minorities existed in Japan, although any human rights problems were still denied. Despite this denial, both Ryukyuans and Ainu tend to be discriminated against as are Burakumin.

The Korean minority is a residue of Japan's colonization of Korea from the early twentieth century until 1945. The Koreans are the only substantial Japanese minority presenting an international dimension, since many of them retain ties or contacts with either of the two Korean states, and their treatment in Japan is often affected by the regional relations of Japan and the two Koreas.

The links between Koreans in Japan and the Korean states gives Koreans resident in Japan their place in the Japanese hierarchical world. Japanese mainstream political consciousness has always ranked all peoples along lines comparable with Japan's own social hierarchy. The Japanese insist on their own uniqueness and do not necessarily regard others as inferior, but judge them in terms of perceived achievement. Successful Western countries rate high, but Asian societies seen as less successful than Japan rate lower. Koreans are ranked rather low, both because of their former status as Japan's colonial subjects and, because of the current state of their homeland, divided between a Stalinist regime in the north and in the south, what was seen as a frequently turbulent, despised client of the United States. South Korea's improved economic clout since the 1960s has won only qualified recognition in Japan's hierarchy of nations.

There are many other smaller minorities in Japan. The number of foreign workers, both legal and illegal, is well in excess of a million men and women coming from most of the countries of east, south-east, and south Asia. Listed by type of employment, illegal women workers are mainly hostesses, factory workers, prostitutes, dishwashers, and waitresses. Illegal men workers are mainly construction and factory workers. Here is the making of a new sub-caste, giving the Koreans and Burakumin a group below them on the social scale.

The small Chinese minority in Japan, about 80,000 settled residents, with 60,000 more temporary residents, mainly students, gives a total of around 140,000 in 1990, does not really fit into the hierarchy. Although they come mainly from Japan's former colonial territories in Taiwan and Manchuria, they tend to derive some degree of status by association with mainland China which, despite its material poverty, is ranked relatively highly because of its cultural legacy to Japan and its weight in international affairs. One index of their different status from Koreans is the more widespread use of Chinese names (83 percent), while most Koreans (91 percent) use Japanese aliases by way of 'passing' as Japanese in order to avoid discrimination.

Other foreign minorities in Japan as of 1990 were Filipinos 43,000, Americans 36,000 (including an unknown number of ethnic Japanese), Brazilian 34,000 (mostly ethnic Japanese), British 9,700, Thai 6,300 and all others 68,800.

The Burakumin

Within Japan, the study of minority issues throws light on the peculiarities of Japanese society as a whole. Among the other minorities, the status and activities of the Burakumin have the most direct bearing on those of the Korean community. The two causes have sometimes shared facilities, for example, when the Buraku Emancipation League in Kyoto helped in the Korean community's efforts on behalf of compensation for 'comfort women'—Korean women procured for sexual service to the wartime Japanese armed forces. See my study, *The Comfort Women,* for more details on this topic.

In 1974, when I was living in Kyoto, I read the classic study of the Burakumin, *Japan's Invisible Race* by De Vos and Wagatsuma, and then used the book as guide to visit several of the nineteen Buraku communities in Kyoto. On my first visit to one of these areas I became lost, and on asking directions, I was informed that the Burakumin had been legislated out of existence at the beginning of the Meiji era, so that my visit was almost a century too late. In fact, I was already within a hundred yards of a Burakumin community which I found was exactly as described in De Vos. Very prominent were the butcher shops which sold fried tripe as well as other organ meats. These shops are a distinctive feature of Buraku communities. Japanese consider a taste for this fried tripe, or any other organ meats, to be repugnant and a generally abhorred Buraku characteristic.

The origins of a class of untouchables or outcasts in Japan lie shrouded in the past, before the beginning of written records. It is probable that concepts of pollution in indigenous Shinto beliefs were reinforced by Buddhist concepts relating to impurities attending the killing of animals and the eating of meat.

6

Taboos against eating meat were established in Japan by the eighth century and certain occupations involved in killing animals and preparting and preparing animal products were thought to be contaminating. These occupations were carried out by defiled, hereditary specialists. By the early eighth century there were already codes which prohibited marriage between freemen and slaves of specified occupations. Although slavery was later abolished, the contaminating nature of certain occupations, combined with marital proscriptions, continued down the centuries.

Among the outcast communities, some were more equal than others. The higher in status of the two classes of despised citizens were the *hinin* or non-people. They were a mixed bunch of beggars, prostitutes, entertainers, and fugitives from justice who, one way or another, had dropped out of the four class feudal ranking of warriors, farmers, artisans, and merchants. For *hinin* there was still hope: if they settled down in normal communities they could revert to human status.

Beneath the *hinin* were a truly wretched class of hereditary outcasts known as *eta* or 'much filth.' *Eta* status was inherited through birth, just as Burakumin status continues to be handed down today. Traditionally the *eta* performed tasks that were considered to be ritually polluting such as animal slaughter and the disposal of the dead. But no change of occupation could save the *eta* who were thought to be genetically subhuman.

For many centuries ordinary Japanese were not only prohibited from marrying *eta* but also had to avoid physical contact with them. They were the true untouchables. In the early 1870s, the new Meiji government abolished the terms *eta* and *hinin* and replaced them with a new euphemism, which in turn was replaced with the more neutral Burakumin, or 'citizens of special communities.' The so-called emancipation of the Burakumin harmed rather than helped them. They continued to be relegated to 'unclean' work such as garbage collection and street sweeping while at the same time they lost their monopoly over the more lucrative leather crafts industry.

Although the law towards the Burakumin has changed for the better, Burakumin remain subject to discrimination as illustrated by the following examples spanning the last century and a half. In a famous case in 1859, an *eta* youth tried to enter a Shinto shrine in Edo (Tokyo) and was beaten to death by the residents of the district. Instead of bringing the guilty to justice, the magistrate responded, 'The life of an *eta* is worth about one-seventh of the life of a townsman. Unless seven *eta* have been killed, we cannot punish a single townsman.' This sort of legal decision has been inconceivable since the early 1870s, but that public attitudes have not in fact changed is suggested by the following three incidents that occurred around 1900, 1960, and 1989.

The historian Hane Mikiso points out that in the minds of the majority of Japanese, the *eta* have long been considered 'lowly, despicable people who deserved to be oppressed. They were seen as dirty, vulgar, smelly, untrust-

7

worthy, dangerous, treacherous, subhuman creatures. In a typical interaction, around the turn of the century, an *eta* was taunted by his fellow students and his teacher. "Isn't it true that you *eta* have no testicles and that you are short of one rib?" They then caught hold of him and stripped his clothes off to examine him.'

George De Vos (1993) tells an illuminating story (from around 1960) about a cobbler, still a Burakumin trade. Once, when the cobbler's son 'delivered shoes to a customer, the money was given to him tied on the end of a bamboo pole—an ancient way of avoiding being "unclean" on the part of those needing the services of outcasts in Kyoto.'

In a recent example, the Buraku Liberation Research Institute gives an account of a message that was circulated by electronic mail to about 30,000 personal computer users on 15 July 1989. 'If you believe nuclear power plants are dangerous, build them in Buraku areas. Or build them in Korea and have them transmit electricity by cable.' Buraku people have been called *eta* and *hinin* and denied treatment as human beings. 'They are not human beings and they don't deserve human rights. They deserve to be killed. Nuclear power plants are not really threatening enough for them. Nuclear testing sites would be more appropriate. Kill them. Yotsu, [four-legged, is a derogatory term for Burakumin], *Eta, Hinin, Chonko* [derogatory for Koreans]. You are all shit.'

The Burakumin's political tactics have provided models for Korean community action. Their pre-war National Levelers Association (Suiheisha) adopted the strategy of public denunciation of cases of discrimination and demands for apology. In 1935, an officially sanctioned Reconciliation Council attempted to improve their condition, in the course of which 5,365 ghetto localities were identified throughout Japan. This list was, however, later misused to provide blacklists to screen out prospective employees and marriage partners. During the 1970s, the League forced apologies from companies found to be using such blacklists, but the practice does not seem to have stopped. The League has been successful in pressuring publishers into deleting any mention of their community from publications of any kind, even when not unfavorable. In 1969, a Special Integration Measures Law resulted in considerable spending by local authorities on housing, schools, community centers, and antidiscriminatory education. However, reflecting the conservative establishment's aversion to social engineering, no antidiscrimination legislation has eventuated and the community continues to be marked by poor school performance, delinquency, involvement with the *Yakuza* criminal underworld, prostitution, and welfare dependency.

The Koreans

The case of the Korean community poses a wide range of issues. Whereas other minorities have Japanese nationality and at least formal legal equality, including the vote, freedom from deportation, and full social welfare, the 700,000 non-naturalized Koreans have few of these rights. Moreover, since naturalization procedures demand a very high degree of cultural assimilation, many have preferred to preserve elements of their cultural heritage and identity, despite the humiliation that this sometimes entails.

A Korean Professor, resident in Japan and quoted by Korean rights activist Yumi Lee, has written:

> Koreans live all over the world and are especially concentrated in the former USSR, China, and Japan, as a consequence of Japan's colonization policies. The phenomenon of Korean immigrants in the United States is a relatively recent thing . . . . Those who live in China and the former USSR have high ethnic consciousness, and have their own newspapers, TV, and radio stations. Koreans in the USA are equally conscious of their ethnicity and unlike the Koreans in Japan have no sense of inferiority. Those who freely emigrated to America would obtain American nationality with gratitude. The treatment of Koreans in Japan has been different. The historical background is completely different. For thirty-six years [under colonialism] Koreans were deprived of their nationality. [That is, Korean nationality ceased to exist.] Although forced to migrate to Japan, Japanese nationality was then unilaterally stripped away [following the Japan-US Peace Treaty]. . . . To survive and live in Japan, some obtained Japanese nationality; they went through an inhuman procedure [discussed below] and are known as 'new Japanese.'

Although some of those who are naturalized in Japan assimilate fully and lose all identity as ethnic Koreans, many of them and even their children find it impossible to reconcile themselves to this. Thus, while other minorities such as Burakumin, Ainu, and Okinawans, represent subcultures within Japanese culture, the Korean case involves the clash of two historically rich and long-established cultures. It is a curiously complex picture.

The Japanese colonization of Korea is sometimes contrasted with that of Western colonial empires, in that it involved a colony that was close by and of related culture, whereas the latter involved remote regions of totally different and often technologically less developed cultures. The great exception in the Western case is, of course, Ireland—and the parallels with the Korean case are striking. In both cases the subject people were deprived of much of their land, driving them to emigrate in large numbers both to the conquering country and elsewhere. Culturally, the native Irish language was largely eliminated, while in Korea the modern education system introduced under colonialism was based on Japanese. The use of the Korean language in education was virtually phased out by World War II. The Koreans sometimes speak of being 'robbed of their language,' though in contrast with the Irish, the Korean language survived intact, in part because of the relative brevity of Japanese rule. The Korean language has, however, been largely eliminated as a functioning written and spoken language among Koreans in Japan, despite the great efforts to preserve it in the schools run by the pro-North Korea group.

Despite the substantial loss of their native language, both Koreans in Japan and the Irish retain distinctive social characteristics. The traditional British stereotypes of the Irish involved traits like stubborn resistance to authority (being 'agin it'), internal divisiveness, impulsiveness, pugnacity, and irrationality. These stereotypes approached so closely to the stereotypes of Koreans among the Japanese that earlier in this century the British (Japan's staunch backers in its earlier expansionist phase) described Koreans as 'the Irishmen of the East.'

Stereotypes of course do not carry us very far. There is, however, a searching and stimulating study on contrastive Japanese and Korean psychology available which illuminates the endemic underlying friction pervading relations between the two peoples. Professor Kim Yang-gi is a Japanese-born Korean comparative ethnologist who is well placed to view both societies from the inside. His title 'Japanese Compared to *Noh* Masks' refers to the difficulty constantly experienced by Koreans in fathoming the feeling or opinions of the much more reserved Japanese. The masks used in the classic Noh drama, an austere product of samurai culture, are carved with great subtlety and may convey a wealth of emotions according to the posture, situation, and understanding of the viewer.

The extent to which the Japanese employ restraint or obliqueness of expression varies according to class or region but is highly developed in the workplace. In a great variety of Japanese social activities, communication appears to be almost telepathic. 'Group action among Japanese sometimes seems to operate by automatic consensus,' writes Kim. 'The group operates spontaneously, without need to explain, as if all act by sizing up each other's inclination telepathically.'

Japanese conferences, for example, tend to be quiet affairs, conclusions being tacitly reached without much controversy. By contrast, Korean conferences tend to be noisy and heated, suggesting a love of controversy, though there is little tendency to nurse resentments after a forthright exchange. In another context, Japanese funerals too are quiet affairs, while at a Korean funeral, the unrestrained expression of grief is perfectly proper. This is only one of the many instances of the Korean preference for giving vent to emotions as opposed to the Japanese way of disciplining or controlling feelings.

Among the Japanese, the sense of social obligation is so strong that where one fails in his duty, suicide is regarded as an honorable response. However, suicide has never had a positive value among Koreans. Their view is that it is our duty to the gods, who have bestowed life on us, to fulfill our destiny,

10

whatever that may be. Kim describes Koreans as 'optimistic fatalists,' still much under the influence of Chinese divination by cycles, symbolized by the *Yin-Yang* and trigram signs on the South Korean flag. Koreans tend to be optimists. In their belief system, there is certain to be a turn for the better, sooner or later. And whereas in drama, ancient or modern, Japanese hold tragedy in high esteem, Korean drama has always insisted on happy endings.

According to Kim, the Japanese perception that Koreans are less totally committed to the group, or less conformist or predictable, is part of the reason non-naturalized Koreans are usually excluded from employment in Japanese corporations of the kind where lifetime employment has been customary. (Even naturalized Koreans sometimes still face employment difficulties.) This perception also keeps Koreans from obtaining public employment where policy questions are decided.

Kim makes a thorough study of how the premodern condition of both countries has influenced modern society. Under its classic form of feudalism, Japan was divided into largely autonomous domains which in an earlier period commonly fought each other militarily but later competed economically, giving rise to urban commercial centers where the merchant class reproduced the hierarchical structures of the samurai. Korea, on the other hand, was a unitary monarchy on the Chinese model, administered by a similar scholar-gentry class, the Yangban, whose main qualification was the classic Confucian education, while their immediate loyalty was to the clan. The Korean structure, and the Chinese, was much less adaptable to modern exigencies than the Japanese case, says Kim. In Japan, a continuing, though not hereditary, establishment has so far succeeded in remolding a traditional ethos to changing situations but is little inclined to entertain any fundamental reorientation of hierarchical values.

Kim's general picture is paralleled by the conclusions of George De Vos, a life-long student of minority issues, in *Social Cohesion and Alienation: Minorities in the United States and Japan* (published in 1993). Describing the Korean community as a 'caste-like minority,' he sees them as victims of 'stringent expectations concerning self-controlled behavior.' Those Koreans most affected by their vulnerable social situation may suffer further loss of morale by seeing the Japanese as more successful practitioners of the Confucian virtues shared by both. He makes generalizations about Koreans with broken marriages, delinquent offspring, and inferior vocations in their more depressed communities. Koreans are less able to make a Japanese-style emotional commitment to organizations, he says, being more competitive than cooperative and prone to factionalism. Ad hoc spells of activism are common among Koreans but, although sometimes successful, are more expressive of identity than purely instrumental. To some extent, activist protests are ends in themselves regardless of whether anything is achieved.

Japanese expressions of popular prejudice against Koreans include a perception of their association with Japanese Leftists or other dissidents; association with *yakuza* and illegal or marginal pursuits, such as their prominence in the *pachinko* (pinball) industry; accusations of allegiance to Korean regimes, particularly in the North; and their alien dietary habits, including the ample use of garlic and organ meats such as liver, heart, and kidneys. Professor Kim also illustrates the contrast between Japanese and Korean temperaments by the homely comparison of lightly flavored Japanese pickles with the Korean *kimchi*, made with garlic and chili.

Yumi Lee provides anecdotal illustrations from her experience.

Recently, an increased number of wealthy high schools take students overseas on school trips. [At that time] Japanese students held a red-covered passport. Students registered as South Korean have a dark green passport. (Those registered as North Korean cannot have passports because Japan and North Korea do not have diplomatic relations).

On the day they leave Japan, all the Korean students are nervous, worrying about their difference being revealed. The teachers are careful. They make red covers for the Koreans passports. The procedure at immigration for foreigners is different from Japanese. Teachers separate the students. The Japanese students go through immigration chatting, excited. Teachers make an excuse for the Korean students and tell the Japanese: 'they are not feeling well and will come a little later.' The Korean students quietly go through immigration by themselves.

Also: I worked for an English conversation school for about four years and introduced myself as Yumi Lee. No one ever asked me any questions about my identity. One day I was asked to teach as a replacement, in a children's class. When I introduced myself, something immediately changed in the atmosphere of the room.

Sometime later I met the regular teacher of the class I taught as a substitute. She said, 'thank you for taking over my class the other day. The students told me that they enjoyed your class very much. One of the students asked me "why is her name Lee?" I replied "Ms Lee is a Korean." She said: "You are kidding! Is she a Korean? I thought she was a nice teacher!" So I asked "Why do you say that?" She said, "Because my dad always says that Koreans are rascals."

2 What it means to be a Korean in Japan

The Korean community's view of its situation in Japan is conditioned by collective recollections of experiences over the better part of this century, since the colonization of their homeland. Yumi Lee's knowledge of her family history, though fragmentary, is typical of many.

A personal story

For the first twenty years of my life my name was Uno Yumi and I did not even know that I had a Korean name. My father is Uno Yukio, my mother Keiko. I later came to know that my parents' given names were Japanised Korean names [i.e. written with the same Chinese characters but pronounced in Japanese].

When I was very young my father drove a ten-ton dump truck. I did not have much opportunity to spend time with him; he took off before the sun rose and came home late at night. He drove from Miyazu [on the coast north of Kyoto] to various towns and cities in the Kansai area. At first, he worked with his brothers in Uno Trading, a family enterprise, but because of personality clashes he broke away and established Uno Building Materials.

My mother is a strong and determined woman. She moved to Miyazu from Kyoto when she married. She managed shops and *okonomiyaki* [a type of pizza cooked at the table] restaurants as well as bringing up four daughters. My mother was born in Korea in 1936 and taken to Sakhalin [an island north of Japan] when she was an infant in 1937. Along with tens of thousands of other Koreans, my mother's father was drafted to Sakhalin by the Japanese and forced to work in the coal mines where the harsh conditions hastened his death.

My maternal grandmother was called Im Yong-nyo. She was born on 10 December 1910. My grandfather was called Pak Jae-kyu, and was

13

born in the same year, the year that Japan colonized Korea. My maternal grandparents, who were both Catholic, were married in 1930, when they were twenty years old. They had four children: two boys and then two girls.

I pressed my mother for more information about the death of her father. She said that she remembered one snowy day in Sakhalin (in the winter of 1943 or 1944) when Japanese mine officials came to her family's door. They handed my grandmother a box containing my grandfather's ashes. This was the first she knew that he had died. She ran out of the house and wept in the snow. She was left alone with four small children whom she brought to Japan, since there was nothing to return to in Korea.

In Japan, my grandmother, who knew next to no Japanese, struggled to survive. The Japanese did not pay her a cent for the death of her husband. She was forced to sell rice on the black market [a common means of survival among Koreans after World War II]. When she was caught by the police, they kicked and slapped her.

My paternal grandfather, like hundreds of thousands of other Koreans, had his land seized and, facing starvation, moved to Japan to survive. According to my father, he used to sell rice crackers and malt candy to support his family. As is still the case today, the *yakuza* Mafia terrorized street vendors, and my grandfather was frequently driven off the street and into brewing shochu [grain or potato spirits]. He saved money bit by bit. He used to say: 'It takes no time to spend money.' With his savings he bought a small mountain forest lot and went into the timber business. It was successful and he became the owner of a mill which was eventually taken over by my father and his brothers.

When my father was small, verbal abuse of Koreans was common: 'You stink like a Korean' he was taunted. He would fight back, but his teacher would force my father to apologize for starting a fight. My father and his brothers were also never allowed to attend the neighborhood children's festivals.

Yumi Lee's parents, following her father's reasonably successful start in business in provincial Miyazu, experienced much improved circumstances after moving to Kyoto at about the time she completed primary school. When first in Kyoto, her father tried his hand at money-lending but, as she put it, he was not 'tough enough' to succeed in this. Because he was a Korean, most employment avenues were closed to him. The license to become a real estate agent did not, however, require Japanese nationality. Eventually, he passed the examination and was awarded a real estate agent's license.

The 1970s and 1980s were good times to be in real estate in Japan and operating from home under their Japanese alias because business contacts could not tell that the salesman was not Japanese. Business boomed and Yumi Lee's parents were able to give her and her three sisters a good education and comfortable lifestyle.

Yumi Lee's mother has some good memories of her Japanese neighbors. 'There were some neighbors who were Japanese who were kind to us. Their warm consideration touched my heart even when I was small. They gave us food and lent us money without any guarantee that the loans would be returned.'

An ironic twist for Koreans who live in Japan is the way they are viewed in Korea. Yumi Lee points out: 'In Korea, we [the community in Japan] are looked down upon because we live in Japan. Members of our own community look down on others who are less successful. Discrimination also exists among Koreans depending on one's place of origin in Korea.'

Official policies regarding education

Official policies which now apply to the Korean community are particularly resented because they recall aspects of colonial policy. Most Korean children attend Japanese schools for two reasons. One, official policies discourage the development of Korean schools (that is, there are just no Korean schools near to where many Koreans live) and, two, private schools face difficulty providing qualification for entry to higher education. To some Koreans in Japan, this situation recalls the education system based on Japanese language and values introduced into Korea under Japanese rule. This system was aimed at complete assimilation and the destruction of Korean national identity and was widely resented. As the Japanese Governor-General's policy statement put it at the outset:

> The relationship between the Empire's homeland and Korea is quite distinctive [as compared with Western colonial empires] in that the territories are adjacent and races identical, so that there is scarcely any obstacle to their fusion and assimilation. Whereas our Empire, by grace of successive sage rulers, has rapidly progressed to high prosperity, Korea has unfortunately been left behind in the march of the times and fallen into decadence. Now that the two countries have been joined into one household, the distinction between fore-runner and laggard inevitably arises.

This was Japan's version of the European colonialists' 'white man's burden.' Some of the Korean intelligentsia accepted total assimilation as the only way to modernize Korean society. One of the number of Korean writers who successfully took up writing in Japanese early expressed the view that this course was inevitable because Japanese was becoming a language of world significance whereas Korean, if it survived, would remain provincial. Gaelic, he pointed out, had been gradually lost in Ireland, and writers like Shaw or Yeats would be unknown if they had written in that language rather than English. Nevertheless, resistance to Japanization was widespread, and some of the Korean community in Japan continue to resist.

Alien Registration

Added to assimilation are the onerous requirements of Alien Registration, which for a long period involved compulsory fingerprinting even for permanent residents. Koreans in Japan are still required to carry a registration card at all times. This requirement parallels the pre-war compulsory membership in the Kyowakai (Concordia Association). This succeeded an earlier welfare organization called the Soaikai (Mutual Devotion) which had been established by the Koreans themselves in 1921. It had been given official funding and recognition by the Japanese authorities, largely as a means of controlling any radical tendencies in the community, whether from Left-wing Japanese trade unions organizing among laborers or Marxist leanings fashionable at the time among the intelligentsia.

In 1936, in the context of a mounting world economic and social crisis and a growing need for Korean labor in Japan, the functions of this Korean association were taken over by the official Kyowakai, and its role was then extended to a policy of all-out assimilation. Associations, headed by the governor, with the police chief and director of education as deputies, were set up in each prefecture in Japan. These were embraced in a Central Kyowakai Headquarters in 1939 and provided benefits such as welfare, employment, and adult education.

Use of Japanese names

The most intensely resented of the colonial hangovers is the pressure to ac Japanese names, not only for naturalization but also for employment. The implications of this complex emotional minefield are discussed in more detail later in this book. Japanese names were first applied to Koreans migrating to Japan, voluntarily or otherwise. Considerations were at first practical rather than ideological, stemming in the first place from the difficulties Japanese have with Korean names. Names in both Korean and Japanese are written in Chinese characters, but the same character is pronounced quite differently. (This is because Koreans pronounce Chinese characters in a manner derived from an archaic form of Chinese while the Japanese pronounce them in an indigenous form, keeping only the meaning of the characters. Even when a Japanese pronunciation is derived from the Chinese, it is another form of archaic Chinese from that used in Korea.) It made things simpler for the Japanese if Koreans abandoned their Korean names and adopted Japanese ones.

Another practical problem is the extremely limited number of Korean names. Korean surnames are virtually identical with Chinese clan names and, as with Chinese, are few in number. One dictionary gives an apparently complete list of 286. Most Koreans in practice share only a handful of names while Japanese surnames are vastly more numerous and are usually derived from localities.

The Koreans overcame this problem in Korea by qualifying their names according to the origin of particular lineages, such as the Chinhae Kims and the Posong Os. Once again, however, the Japanese argued that Japanese names were more practical even in Korea itself. By the late 1930s, however, these practical arguments were overwhelmed by the ideological: the aims were assimilation and the destruction of Korean identity. This was vividly demonstrated by the launching on 11 February 1940 of the program to impose Japanese names on all Koreans. This program was coincidental with the 2,600th anniversary of the legendary founding of the Japanese imperial line.

Koreans deeply resented these Japanese policies because they clashed with time-honored traditions. The Koreans had had clan names for as far back as their history was recorded, whereas in Japan, until the abolition of feudalism, only certain privileged groups were allowed surnames. Moreover, contrary to Japanese practice, in the strict Confucian custom followed in Korea, people of the same clan name could not marry, while women entering a clan through marriage kept their own clan name. Adoptions were restricted to within the same clan. Japanese policy thus cast aside millennia of tradition.

Despite Korean resistance, Japanese threats, discrimination, and harassment according to Kim Il-myon succeeded in forcing 76 percent of the population by mid-1940 to adopt Japanese names. The process was only halted after some months when members of the former Korean royal house, now enrolled among the Japanese peerage, raised protests at the court level to which their rank gave access. They had retained their own clan name Yi (also rendered as Lee).

A personal story

Yumi Lee relates her family's recollection of this re-naming process:

> The family name Kim which means 'gold' or 'money' in Chinese characters, was transformed into Kanemura (gold village) or Kanai (gold well), leaving some trace of the real name. On the other hand, my grandparents' family name Lee was changed completely, to Uno. When I asked my father the reason, he told me that an official came over to the house with a list of Japanese names and my grandfather had to choose

17

one from the list. Some outraged Koreans protested by choosing vulgar words for their names.

Since the amendment of the Domicile Registration Law in 1984, Japanese officialdom no longer insists on the adoption of Japanese names when Koreans are naturalized. Most however, do adopt Japanese names in order to avoid discrimination. Most Koreans in Japan use Japanese aliases as a means of getting by but regard the need to do so as evidence of a continuing Japanese colonialist mentality. Yumi Lee writes:

> Those people whom I met in the last ten years know me as Yumi Lee; my friends whom I met before the age of twenty know me as Yumi Uno. I take Yoga classes where I am known as Uno in one class, and Lee in the other. I get confused between the two. It is almost a joke. I introduce myself as Lee when I want that person to know who I really am. When I want to maintain a distance I use Uno. When I make a phone call, I sometimes cannot remember which name I have used.

Loyalty oaths

Another problem for Koreans regarding naturalization is the need to swear allegiance to the Japanese Constitution. Although the post-war constitution is based on popular sovereignty, it still describes the Emperor as symbol of the nation, and indeed the same Emperor who presided over Korea's colonial subjugation, from 1925 to 1945, continued on the throne for nearly half a century following Japan's defeat. To many in the Korean community, as well as Japanese dissidents, whether Left-wing, religious, feminist, or other, the Emperor is the focus of resentments against all forms of oppression.

All these factors help to explain why many Korean residents in Japan regard naturalization and assimilation as 'treason' and that to naturalize means that the Korean in Japan has accepted and internalized the low estimate most Japanese hold of Koreans. To the extent that discrimination is also viewed as partly intended to force assimilation, to naturalize under these circumstances represents a surrender to pressure alien to the Korean character.

Weak ties to the homeland

With the passage of time, ties to Korea, for Koreans in Japan, have weakened. Already three generations of Koreans have been born in Japan, with only 7 percent of their community born in Korea. Those born in Korea were almost all born in the South. Although those affiliated with North Korea maintain a generally firm allegiance to that state, owing mainly to their extensive ethnic education system, opportunities to visit the North are much more limited than to the South, with which Japan has very close relations. When younger members of Southern affiliated groups visit the South, as their elders encourage them to do, they soon become aware of how alien they appear to the local society and vice versa. Even enthusiastic students of the language often find themselves ill at ease in attempting to use it. Yumi Lee writes:

> My Korean was improving but it never satisfied them. On the other hand when the Japanese stewardesses trained in the same session as I was said simple things like '*annyong haseyo*' (hullo), South Koreans would compliment them. 'That is great! You can speak Korean!' No matter how much effort I made to improve my Korean I was a mere Japan-resident Korean who could not even speak the mother language properly. I learned the bitter lesson that neither Japan nor Korea was my home.

A more extensive account of 'culture shock' (Fukuoka 1991) is given by a young Korean woman named Kim Myong-mi or, in Japanese, Aoi Akemi (written with the same Chinese characters as Myong-mi). She attended weekly Korean lessons in Japan but made little progress. She said that the Korean phonetic script, *hangul* (used like the Japanese script kana as an alternative or auxiliary script), 'made her dizzy.' But her father nevertheless persuaded her to take up a two-year scholarship in South Korea.

During her stay, she experienced three-monthly cycles of fulfillment and homesickness (for Japan). Material satisfaction was well below the Japanese level, and she found communication difficult. Her main difficulty with food was the Korean habit of cooking several days' supply of food at once and keeping it to be served in what she found to be a rather monotonous series of meals, in contrast with the Japanese practice of fresh preparation of each meal. In addition, because of water shortage Koreans bathed only weekly as opposed to the daily baths she was accustomed to in Japan.

Kim worked as a home tutor in Japanese and made friends, but she never felt accepted. Her habitual description as an 'overseas compatriot' (*kyopo*) was used with an air of disdain, and she was thought to be no different from a Japanese. Her biggest satisfaction was the forming of friendships with other Japan-resident Koreans, with whom she could relax completely. This defined for her the essential nature of the community in Japan.

An account of visits to North Korea conveys a similar impression with a different flavor. Pak Yang-ja, a young woman who attended North Korean affiliated schools, including the Korean University, first visited the country with a group of secondary students. On that occasion they were taken only on a scenic tour without contacting the local people. Later, however, in the summer of 1989, she worked with a youth service team in North Korea for two months.

> On this occasion we worked with local people and talked about all sorts of things with them. On making such contact we had a sense of being in our homeland. They could tell at a glance that we had come from Japan if only because we were wearing our school uniforms. We also looked quite Japanese and felt that we were being viewed rather coldly as foreigners. But when we talked with them we felt that even though we had grown up in different surroundings, we had something in common as fellow Koreans. They were all simple and sincere, with a goodness not found in Japan. We were sad on leaving Korea. But I could not live there. I have thought that I might but, considering the poor living standards there . . . if I had been born there it might have been all right. I dislike Japan, but having been born and brought up here, I am inextricably tied to it. My way of thinking is Japanese. Capitalistic modes of thought have completely pervaded my lifestyle. Mine is a half-way existence. (Fukuoka 1991)

The Korean community in Japan is unwilling to lose its identity by complete assimilation into Japanese society, yet largely alienated from the homeland, finds itself in a situation likened to the bats in Aesop's fable, who were accepted neither by birds nor beasts. Yet many in the community are hopeful of maintaining a meaningful identity by creative adaptation to the realities of their situation. In this they are encouraged by the advance of minority rights throughout the world, particularly under the aegis of United Nations groups. Then there is the Japanese government's much proclaimed policy of 'internationalization' aimed at better integrating Japan with the world community. They promote the goal of the community's full acceptance in Japan in terms of 'internationalization from within,' describing themselves as intermediaries in the move towards a more cosmopolitan outlook for Japan.

Legislative gains

As will be described in chapter four, Koreans have used litigation and protest as a means of expanding their rights and, within the limits set by legislation, have secured important gains. These have included recommendations that permanently resident aliens, particularly those born in Japan and fulfilling normal civic duties, should not be lumped in with more transient aliens on the basis of a blanket distinction based on nationality alone. In one case, relating to a protest against compulsory fingerprinting, a judgment reads in part:

20

In considering the human rights of aliens . . . these must be approached multidimensionally in accordance with their concrete situation. Where these fully form a component of Japanese society, fulfilling exactly identical social obligations as nationals such as taxation, it is not permissible to ignore this reality by making a simple classification between nationals and foreigners. (Tanaka 1991)

Such judgments have implied that legislators are remiss in neglecting such issues, and it is certainly true that neither the legislature nor the administration have shown much initiative in such areas. Where improvements have occurred, it has generally stemmed from external pressures such as negotiations with South Korea or international treaties under United Nations auspices.

The recovery of legal rights is not, however, sufficient. Ultimately, the issues of Korean ethnic identity are cultural. In the words of another judgment: 'It is realized that, for Japan-resident Koreans to recover their human status, there is no other way but to retain Korean names, behave as Koreans, learn Korean history, and maintain their pride as Koreans.' One interviewee sums up the Korean cultural heritage as 'language, historical legacy, and cooking.' Another describes the older generations' regret at having lost so much of their cultural heritage in the struggle for survival, though this is combined with the hope that, even if formal ethnic education has its limits, a certain 'Korean sensibility' can be preserved by community action.

3 Divisions in the Korean community: The Soren, the Mindan, the Mintoren

The Osaka 'One Korea Festival' has been held annually from 1985. In 1994, it was extended to Tokyo. But for Koreans in Japan, the idea of 'One Korea' is far from being realized. Divisions within the Korean community persist. First, both in date of origin and ethnic consciousness, though not now in numbers, comes the North Korea affiliated General Association of Korean Residents in Japan, in Japanese the Zai-Nippon Chosenjin Sorengokai, generally abbreviated to Soren. The Korean form of this name, Ch'ongnyon in the McCune-Reischauer system, is generally used with variations in the English language press and spelled Chongryun by the organization itself, but since Japanese is the language most used in the community, it is perhaps best to keep the Japanese forms in this as in the other cases.

The other organization is the South Korea affiliated Korean Residents' Union in Japan, in Japanese the Zai-Nippon Daikan Minkoku Kyoryumindan, abbreviated to Mindan. Here Daikan Minkoku is the Japanese form of South Korea's formal name Taehan Minguk, usually shortened in Japanese to Kankoku. This is preferred in common usage to avoid 'Chosen.' This is felt to have unpleasant associations, though the Soren affiliates continue to use it, following North Korean usage.

Third is a grouping which is oriented more towards the practical needs of the community in Japan. It consists mainly of younger Koreans less tied to the homeland and a considerable number of Japanese activists sympathetic to them and genuinely dedicated to an internationalist ideal. Its main focus is the Liaison Association for Fighting Ethnic Discrimination, abbreviated to Mintoren. As its name indicates, it is not a formalized organization but holds annual conferences and mobilizes support and contributions wherever and whenever issues present themselves.

A fourth type of grouping is formed by the clubs of naturalized Koreans who still wish to preserve their ethnicity. They are called Seiwakai ('realization of harmony'). It is noteworthy that an unofficial sociological survey carried out from South Korea under Min Kwan-sik received more cooperation from these clubs than from the Mindan. Most claimed they had naturalized to spare their descendants the discrimination they themselves had suffered, though in social terms this is not always effective, and a few regret naturalization. Members tend to be business executives or professionals. According to the survey, 46 percent of naturalizing Koreans maintain family traditions and celebrate the yearly round of household festivals of a seasonal or ancestral nature. Those fully assimilating to Japanese ways usually belong to small communities with little group support. These have married Japanese and even support the Japanese side in televised sports contests against Korea.

Finally, there is agreed to be a sizable number of Koreans, estimated at perhaps 50,000, who are either illegal immigrants or who have avoided alien registration. These presumably participate in the life of the Korean community, but little can be said about them.

The nature of the divisions within the Korean community is best described by outlining their history.

The Soren

This represents the present form of a succession of organizations which at first, until the late 1960s, embraced most of the Korean community. It contracted to a solid core of those people most resistant to assimilation or naturalization. They describe themselves as 'overseas citizens' of the Democratic People's Republic of Korea and elect six representatives to its Supreme People's Congress. In the late 1950s, the Soren sponsored a large-scale migration to North Korea, but this has not been repeated, largely because the comparative prosperity attained by its members has enabled them to contribute substantially to their homeland's economy through remittances and investment. This has resulted in frequent distrust and harassment by Japanese officials, so that less militant members of the Korean community prefer the more secure status derived from affiliation to the Mindan and South Korea, or else choosing naturalization.

Late in World War II, when the Japanese government still hoped to fight to a stalemate, the Cabinet sought to secure the firmer allegiance of its colonial subjects by a 'policy to revise the treatment of Koreans and Taiwanese' of a more conciliatory nature. This was to include freedom of travel, equality of wages, and an extension to the colonies of voting rights, hitherto restricted to residents of the Japanese homeland. These measures were aborted by the end of the War, but one interim result was the replacement of the strict control mechanism of the Kyowakai by a more welfare oriented organization called the Koseikai (Welfare Association). Collaborationist Koreans also formed a politically oriented Isshinkai (Unity Association) with a view to taking advantage of the concessions promised by the authorities.

In mid-October 1945, only weeks after the end of the War, an initially non-political umbrella organization was formed to coordinate the interests of the Korean community in the transitional phase of political uncertainty and economic devastation. It was called the Association of Koreans in Japan, in Japanese Zai-Nippon Chosenjin Remmei, abbreviated to Choren. For a time it effectively represented the 2.4 million Koreans in Japan (over one tenth of Korea's population) in negotiations with both the Japanese government and the Occupation forces. It derived a certain status from the initial Occupation policy of regarding former colonial subjects as 'liberated nationals,' though this term was badly defined and soon lost practical significance. Meanwhile, however, the Choren played a positive role.

It took over the premises of the former Government-General of Korea and the Koseikai, handled disputes of any kind between Koreans and Japanese, and was entrusted by the Japanese police with the administration of justice to Korean criminals. It distributed relief supplies obtained from the Welfare Ministry and obtained considerable funds from the Finance Ministry. It was also financed by extracting separation bonuses and back pay from companies that had employed Korean laborers.

Until May 1946, the Choren controlled the trains and ships used in repatriating the great majority of the Koreans in Japan. This program was then taken over by the Occupation and civil authorities. A fairly large minority of Koreans declined the opportunity to return home, mainly because of restrictions on the property that could be taken. This was set at ¥1,000 in cash or equivalent and 250 pounds of personal effects. Although the mass of penniless conscript laborers might not be much affected, this represented a hardship for those Koreans who had obtained some degree of prosperity, and the small class of professionals. In addition, the situation in South Korea was chaotic.

Immediately after Japan's surrender, a Government-General official secretly met an underground nationalist figure, Yo Un-hyong, who had apparently been under surveillance but was now approached for assistance in keeping order until Occupation forces took over. For this purpose Yo secured the release of all political prisoners and organized a Nation Building Preparatory Committee. Most of the long-term resistance leaders were abroad: Kim Koo and the Korean National Provisional Government in Chungking with the Chinese Nationalist Government; Syngman Rhee in the US; the Free Korea Alliance under Kim Tu-bong in Yenan with the Chinese Communists and Kim Il-sung's group in Siberia. Yo hoped to organize a Korean government which could receive returning leaders, without distinction as to affiliation, and forestall a military administration by Occupation forces.

From the beginning, however, Communist sympathizers tended to dominate the Preparatory Committee because, as in Japan itself and indeed everywhere in Axis controlled areas, any resistance movements had been centered on the far Left. By the end of August 1945, local People's Committees had been established throughout Korea which, it is claimed, could have formed the basis of a workable indigenous administration. The 'People's Republic of Korea' was then proclaimed.

By early September, however, Soviet and US forces by prior agreement had divided Korea at the 38th parallel for the purpose of disarming and repatriating all Japanese. For two or three years, the movement of Koreans between the two zones was not much restricted. The Soviet forces established themselves earlier and won initial popularity by a proclaimed policy of allowing the Koreans to control their own destiny. Provisional People's Committees dominated by returning exiles from China and Siberia took over all Japanese facilities and assets.

The US Commander-in-Chief sent to confront them, General Hodge, seems to have regarded Koreans as enemy nationals equal to the Japanese and when told of the 1943 Cairo Declaration promising Korea 'deliverance from slavery' is said to have retorted: 'to hell with the Cairo Declaration!'

On arrival in Seoul he issued a proclamation insisting on immediate obedience to all orders issued under his authority. Having no other source of information on conditions in Korea, he relied on the advice of the Japanese Government-General's administration and retained the services of its Korean officials and police in the military administration that he proceeded to install. These collaborators were deeply unpopular, and reliance on them proved to be a long-term weakness in subsequent South Korean regimes.

When Yo Un-hyong visited General Hodge he found him solely concerned with eliminating Communists. Yo had hoped for a united front of all elements to rebuild Korea, but Hodge rebuffed him and on 10 October proclaimed that the military government was the sole authority in South Korea, refusing any recognition to the 'People's Republic of Korea.' Resistance to the military government, combined with economic dislocation, led to riots and uprisings in many areas, which were suppressed over the next couple of years, involving numerous casualties and thousands of arrests. A South Korean Constabulary, organized in December 1945 and based on former members of the Japanese armed forces, assisted the occupation forces. US servicemen in the region often remarked on the paradox that the occupation of the real former enemy Japan was proceeding so smoothly, while that of liberated Korea was far more troublesome.

Exiled non-Communist leaders like Kim Koo and Syngman Rhee returned but were given little immediate role. Instead, the US government proposed a United Nations Trusteeship of the whole country as the most feasible alternative. This policy was adopted at a US-British-Soviet foreign ministers' conference in Moscow in December 1945, without consulting any Koreans. It provided for a provisional Korean government to be supervised for a maximum of five years by these three powers, with Nationalist China. The plan was vehemently opposed in Korea by a broad front led by Kim Koo. One popular orator declared that Koreans preferred kimchi (Korean pickles, symbolizing self-determination) to either steak (the US) or borsch (the Soviet Union).

In both zones of Korea the proposal was only supported by Communist elements and, although a joint US-Soviet commission for implementing the trusteeship sat in Seoul from March to May 1946, the attempt was abandoned as unworkable. Subsequently both Yo Un-hyong and Kim Koo, among many others, were assassinated, leaving Syngman Rhee to be ultimately installed as the US nominee as President of a separate South Korea.

With Korea in such a condition, many repatriates smuggled themselves back to Japan or carried on an underground traffic across the straits. Population figures are obscure, but when some stabilization was achieved, the registered numbers of Koreans in Japan settled at around two-thirds of a million. This figure has not changed substantially since that time because natural population increase is countered by later repatriation and naturalization.

The Choren soon became more politicized. It had included some assimilationist elements like the Isshinkai, as well as Christian organizations which under colonial conditions had flourished as a kind of alternative to Japanization. The authorities had found these difficult to suppress because of their international backing. But the greater part of the membership tended towards Left-wing radicalism in direct response to long-held resentment of the Japanese establishment. These Left-wing elements had long had underground contacts with Japanese Communists and dissidents, both through the labor movement and intellectual circles. With the abolition of the pre-war system of ideological control under the Special Higher ('Thought') Police, these long hidden alliances could come into the open.

The leading figure was a former political prisoner, Kim Ch'on-hae, also a leading figure of the pre-war underground Communist Party. He had already served seventeen years of a life sentence. According to pre-war ideology, Marxists were the ultimate heretics and could be sentenced to death. However, the Japanese establishment was reluctant to carry out executions, instead preferring brainwashing carried out by the skilled Thought Police.

With the support of the radical mainstream in the Choren, Kim Ch'on-hae became its 'supreme advisor.' He was also a leading member of the Communist Party's central executive committee. Accordingly, the organization rapidly became involved with Communist and other radical activity. Korean activists were sometimes described as the 'advance guard' of the proletarian movement, impelled alike by temperament, earlier experience, and current hardship. Japanese enjoyed preference in employment and many Koreans were forced to survive by black-market trading and illegal distilling. This created tensions with the occupation authorities, especially against the background of the developing Cold War, the division of Korea, and the revival of the Japanese establishment as Asia's 'bulwark against communism.'

Many members of the Choren were alarmed by this radical tendency and broke away to join the Mindan which was formed in late 1948, at about the time that the South Korean government was established, under Syngman Rhee. For many years, the Mindan was not particularly effective, even though it represented the more prosperous section of the community. Although the Mindan maintained relations with Rhee's Mission in Japan, it received little support from him up to his overthrow in 1960. Rather the reverse: the Mission was dependent on the Mindan's help.

The far more dynamic Choren was involved in many campaigns and conflicts including, most memorably, its program of ethnic education and its opposition to laws which restricted property purchases by foreign nationals. The first Korean schools and classes were established, initially with the needs of repatriates in mind, in order to provide basic literacy and general preparation for life in Korea. However, when it became clear that substantial numbers would remain in Japan, the main aim of the schools became the preservation of the Korean heritage in Japan. Despite the extreme hardships of the time, extraordinary efforts were made to promote Korean education. Especially effective was the slogan: 'Let's establish our schools, those with money providing money, those who can labor providing labor, those with knowledge providing knowledge!'

At first the Japanese authorities were disposed to allow aliens to educate their own people rather than burden the Japanese system. They left the status of such schools to be determined by prefectural school boards which had received considerable autonomy under Occupation policy. But later, encouraged by Occupation fears of subversion, the authorities began to revert to earlier policies of assimilation. At the beginning of 1948, the Choren operated 578 schools at four levels, with about 68,000 pupils, and the Mindan operated 54 schools at the two junior levels, with about 6,300 pupils.

At this juncture, at the instance of Occupation General Headquarters, the Education Ministry issued a direction to the prefectures that Korean children must either be enrolled in the public system or in private schools accredited in accordance with the Japanese School Education Law. This meant that curricula would follow standard Japanese lines, and any Korean subjects would be relegated to extra-curricular status. All buildings leased by existing Korean schools had to be evacuated pending application for approved private schools.

Korean education committees attempted to negotiate a compromise so that instruction could be in Korean with Japanese a compulsory subject. The Choren was also willing to accept Occupation censorship of textbooks. The authorities nevertheless rejected the proposed compromise and proceeded to close the schools. The Koreans were resolved to defend their system at any cost. The flash point occurred in the Kansai area where most of the schools were leased, rather than owned, as they were in Tokyo. The outcome was the infamous 'Osaka-Kobe Education Incident' of April 1948.

27

In Osaka, 8,000 Koreans surrounded the Prefectural Office after closure orders had been issued to 19 of the 56 schools in their area. They staged a sit-in to force the governor to negotiate. Four thousand police were mobilized and 180 protesters arrested. Police fired on the demonstrators, and a youth was killed. Soon afterwards in Kobe, violence erupted which the police were unable to contain. A state of emergency was declared for the first and only time under the Occupation. Koreans demanded direct negotiations with the governor but were told he was absent. Finally a crowd forced their way in, found the governor meeting with the police chief and the mayor, and compelled him to sign a proclamation rescinding the local closure orders and releasing protesters arrested earlier.

Lieutenant-General Eichelberger of the United States Eighth Army then took over from the Japanese, reinforcing the local police with military police and canceling the governor's proclamation. Night raids on the Korean quarter resulted in hundreds being injured, vast property damage, and 1,600 arrests, bringing to 4,600 the number detained since the beginning of the dispute. A total of 169 were charged with sedition, while 29, including 10 Japanese, were court-martialed.

The policy outcome was a one-sided compromise with the Ministry of Education whereby ethnic studies could be taught in private schools on a restricted basis. Worse was to come. Late the following year, the Choren was banned under the Organization Control Law and its property confiscated. Ethnic education was then effectively dead. This was the beginning of the so-called 'Red Purge' under which many thousands of Japanese Leftists were dismissed from both public and private employment as part of a general crackdown on presumed subversives, Korean or Leftist, arising from a change in Occupation priorities.

The Cold War had by then produced a radical reorientation in US policies for the occupation. Winston Churchill's 'Iron Curtain' speech of 5 March 1946 had formally ushered in this era of world history, though it had long been foreshadowed in some areas. In Japan, for example, the Emperor's exemption from any prosecution for war guilt, though broadly intended to avoid undue social destabilization, seems to have also involved the consideration that the monarchy presented a barrier to Left-wing radicalism. The full effects of the Cold War were delayed in Japan for two or three years by hopes that the Chinese National regime could contain Communist influence in Asia.

The Occupation's initial aims were broadly defined as demilitarization and democratization. The former embraced the dismantling of all armed forces, trials of the leadership held responsible for the war, and the purge of the upper ranks of politics and the economy under the wartime regime, as well as an ultimately abortive dissolution of the Zaibatsu combines which had facilitated the war mobilization of the economy. Also included was national reeducation, which facilitated democratization. This centered on the new, highly liberal

Constitution and support of the rights of organized labor as a 'countervailing force' to future reactionary trends.

The Occupation authorities were, however, taken aback by the militancy of the labor movement after its long suppression and by its close links with Left-wing political parties, partly Communist but mainly social democratic. This was of course alien to US political traditions as the US and Canada are the only developed nations where labor-based or social democratic parties have been unable to emerge. So in May 1946, 'New Dealer' elements in GHQ held partly responsible for the situation were replaced, while media censorship, originally directed against ultranationalist influences, was extended to suppress Marxist tendencies. In the US itself the New Dealers were defeated in the midterm election in November, giving rise to pressures favoring Japan's economic recovery and rearmament, even at the cost of reform, in order to relieve the financial burden of occupation and the possible defense of Japan against subversion or attack.

The first election under Japan's new Constitution in April 1947 marked the high water mark of social democratic success, with the Socialists emerging as the largest party and ruling in coalition with the Democratic party, a revival of one of Japan's two main parties of the pre-totalitarian era. But a combination of factionalism and corruption brought the collapse of the coalition and the long-term domination of the Liberal Party, heir to the other main pre-war party. This was led throughout by Yoshida Shigeru—antimilitarist but a strongly conservative and monarchist figure who was thoroughly committed to the 'Reverse Course' now being introduced by the occupation.

The change of direction became explicit with National Security Council Report 13/2 of October 1948, which marked the abandonment of war trials, the depurge of the wartime leadership, the abandonment of Zaibatsu dissolution, and Japan's revival as Asia's 'bulwark against communism' to replace the collapsing Nationalist regime in China. The purge of Left-wing elements, inevitably impinging on much of the Korean community, was pursued under the Organization Control Ordinance and the Subversive Activities Prevention Law.

Meanwhile, the Choren had participated in a successful campaign which brought lasting benefits to the Korean community. Their first challenge came about when, as part of this process of economic reconstruction, the government published a draft Ordinance on the Acquisition of Property by Foreign Nationals. Property was defined widely enough to involve all possible aspects of business activities, all of which became subject to a process of application and approval controlled by the Foreign Capital Commission. Pending a peace treaty, the Korean community were still for most purposes regarded as Japanese nationals. They were, however, designated foreign nationals for the purpose of the draft Ordinance. If implemented, this law would open the way to victimization of the Korean community.

The Choren immediately mobilized a widespread protest movement including not only the Korean community but also sympathetic Japanese groups, such as smaller businessmen threatened by the new financial policies, as well as the Overseas Chinese Federation, who enjoyed the advantage of being Allied nationals. They addressed petitions to Occupation authorities and made protests to the Prime Minister and Diet which pointed out that property held by the Korean community could in no way be regarded as foreign capital.

Negotiations with the Commission finally produced the desired result. An amendment was added to the ordinance stating that Koreans who had been of Japanese nationality as of 2 September 1945, the formal date of surrender, and had since resided continuously in Japan, would not be treated as foreign nationals in respect to the law. This ruling has continued to be applied, and allows the Korean community a modest share of Japan's later prosperity.

The Korean War began in mid-1950, only a few months after the dissolution of the Choren. For a time, it seemed possible that this war would lead into a long-term global conflict. Militants in the former Choren resolved to play their part in any struggle and formed an underground United Democratic Front in Japan for the Unification of Korea (in Japanese the Zainichi Chosen Toitsu Minshu Sensen abbreviated to Minsen). It formed a paramilitary Committee for the Defense of the Fatherland which worked with its Communist Japanese counterpart in what was called the 'Molotov Cocktail Era.' This involved the fire-bombing of police stations, sabotage of factories and United States bases and the like, but as the limitations of such tactics became apparent and the war in Korea reached a stalemate, the Communist movement reverted to more normal political activity.

Following the 1952 ratification of the Peace Treaty and the end of the Occupation administration, the new democratic Japanese Constitution took full effect and under its provisions for freedom of association, the Minsen was legalized. For some time it continued to work in close cooperation with the Communist Party, but dissatisfaction gradually mounted. Members accused the leadership of subordinating Korean to Japanese interests (even if these were antiestablishment) and of the 'error of falling into ethnic nihilism.' Members also felt that the Minsen had neglected its primary duty of defense of the fatherland, the DPRK, had lost autonomy, and functioned as a mere component in the 'democratization of Japan.'

Han Dok-su led this protest against the leadership of the Minsen, and his final success was precipitated by a communiqué issued by the North Korean foreign minister Nam Il in early 1955 stating that his government was prepared to enter into normal relations with Japan. Even the Minsen's Japanese Communist allies realized that, if Koreans were to continue in the joint struggle against the Japanese government, they would become an obstacle to North Korea's efforts to normalize diplomatic relations. So after some further intensive debate, the Minsen was dissolved and replaced by the Soren, with Han as its chairman. From 1964, it formally presented itself as an organization of overseas nationals of the DPRK which, in this capacity, would avoid interfering in Japan's internal politics and practice lawful activities only.

The Soren carefully hewed to these stated policies, even refraining as much as possible from accepting the limited state welfare benefits available to Koreans and avoiding official participation in the campaign against the fingerprinting of foreign nationals. Therefore, Japanese authorities came to recognize the Soren as not subversive, and they relaxed some of their surveillance.

The Soren introduced a comprehensive network of support among the community, embracing youth, women's, educational, Buddhist, and writers' organizations, together with active media organizations. There were 2,300 full-time activists at the outset. By the end of the decade, something like 70 percent of the Koreans in Japan were affiliated with the Soren. Han Dok-su remained chairman into the 1990s and enjoyed something of the semi-deification of North Korea's Chairman Kim Il-sung. Although a democratic election should be held for the post of Chairman and other Central Committee offices at each three year congress, Han Dok-su's position has never been challenged. A vote is taken on a show of hands, upon which the candidates are selected by top-down appointment based on loyalty to the leader and faith in the organization.

The mid-1950s were a favorable time to make a start on promoting North Korean interests. The Korean War had ended in 1953 and relations between Japan and South Korea were poor throughout the decade. Syngman Rhee's regime proclaimed that South Korea's territorial waters extended sixty miles from the coast, at a time when three miles was the standard in international law. For some years, Japanese fishermen found within the Rhee line were imprisoned and their vessels confiscated. Completely unrealistic reparations were demanded as a pre-condition for regular diplomatic relations, and additional friction was generated by indiscreet remarks from the Japanese side that Japan's rule in Korea had been legal and had benefited the Koreans.

Soon after Nam Il's communiqué in 1955, an unofficial Japanese mission visited Pyongyang to explore possibilities. This was followed by an initial agreement in 1957 with Japanese trading interests, while the Soren established a DPRK-Japan Trade Association in its headquarters.

The Soren's main project in the late 1950s was, however, a major repatriation program to North Korea, aimed at assisting its post-war reconstruction and development. Although the great majority of Korean residents had originated from areas now in South Korea, they felt no attachment to the Rhee regime, which had always neglected their interests on the pretext that they were the Japanese government's responsibility. While South Korea looked very much a client state of the United States, Soren propaganda successfully presented the North as the true embodiment of national identity. This impression was strengthened by massive contributions from the DPRK to the Korean

Education Assistance Fund, which initiated a revival of the ethnic education program, largely dormant since its earlier suppression.

In late 1958, the North Korean government undertook to bear the travel costs of all who might wish to repatriate to Korea. This offer won the Soren widespread support in Japan, including both leading figures in the ruling Liberal Democratic Party, as well as the Socialist and Communist Parties, not to mention local administrations throughout the country. Japanese of all stripes were keen to get rid of the Koreans, so ending the problems caused by this troublesome minority. At the highest level, the Japanese government realized that such untrammeled enthusiasm to get rid of the Koreans might not amuse the United States, let alone South Korea. The solution was highly imaginative packaging, whereby what amounted to ethnic cleansing was presented as a humanitarian program invoking the Universal Declaration of Human Rights on the freedom to choose one's domicile.

Not surprisingly, the South Korean government protested vigorously, attempting vainly to enlist United States support and threatening to use its naval forces to intercept any repatriation ships bound for North Korea. In Japan, the Mindan launched a counter campaign against 'forced labor recruitment' for North Korea, lobbying politicians and agitating against repatriation within the Korean community. But this proved ineffective. The Mindan finally blamed its failure on the Rhee regime's indifference to the welfare of the community, leaving them open to the blandishments of the North with its offer of a share in the benefits of its 'workers' paradise.' With assistance from the Red Cross, about 100,000 Koreans (including 1,831 Japanese wives) were repatriated to North Korea over an eight year period.

It is interesting to reflect that these Koreans went to North Korea at roughly the same time and in roughly similar numbers that Chinese Indonesians moved to their own 'workers' paradise' in China. Much is known about their unhappy experience in China (most left China when allowed, only to be stranded in Hong Kong), but almost nothing is known about the repatriates to North Korea, except for a tantalizing glimpse in 1994, when the brother of one of the Japanese wives visited her in North Korea and reported on the primitive living conditions there.

As with its predecessor, the Choren, the Soren has been involved in a long series of campaigns and disputes. It has also continued the strategy of working closely with Left-wing parties, and the Japanese Socialist party was its favorite ally in recent years.

The largest and most disastrous campaign for the Soren was its opposition to the Republic of Korea-Japan Normalization Treaty. In 1960, the fall of Syngman Rhee and the subsequent rise of the military dominated regime of Park Chung-Hee opened the door to the normalization of relations with Japan. Unlike Rhee, who neither knew nor cared about economics, Park could see that stable relations with Japan were essential for Korea's economic progress.

Also unlike Rhee, Park had close links with Japan and had been an officer in the Japanese army. He was willing to make concessions in return for economic aid and formal diplomatic recognition of his regime.

The Soren and the Japanese Left Wing opposed these negotiations, partly because Japan's recognition of one Korean state would tend to perpetuate the division of the Peninsula and partly because it would re-open the south to Japanese exploitation. The Left Wing for its part opposed any move suggestive of a return to expansionist policies which in the past had been so closely linked to the suppression of dissidence. Added to this in the current context was Japanese identification with the western camp in the Cold War, to which the Left Wing opposed its doctrine of unarmed neutrality, in accordance with the renunciation of war in the new Constitution, ironically imposed by the occupation in its early reforming phase.

The Soren dispatched propaganda teams to 249 cities in Japan, while massive street demonstrations were repeatedly held in Tokyo. This time, however, care was taken to avoid violence. Many Mindan affiliates also participated in demonstrations outside the Korean mission and hotels occupied by the ROK representatives, their objection being directed at the humiliatingly conciliatory approach being made to negotiations, as well as the exclusion of Mindan from the talks. In South Korea, the opposition to the Normalization Treaty was so strong that martial law had to be imposed for the signing of the treaty.

As the talks neared their climax an immense groundswell of Japanese opposition to negotiations swamped the Koreans' voices. In 1965, 2,000,000 demonstrators protested in 2,900 locations. Japanese opposition was fired partly by the anti-war movement, which argued that the proposed treaty would lead to a military alliance with a South Korea already involved in the Vietnam War. This was held to threaten wider entanglements for Japan, leading to the revival of Right wing ideology and militarism. But despite widespread public disquiet, the treaty passed in the Diet, the Japanese parliament, where the Liberal Democratic party enjoyed a majority in both Houses. The Democratic Socialist Party, which consistently backed Japan's alignment with the West, also supported this treaty.

The treaty, among other things, established the Mindan as a serious rival to the Soren. It now became an agency of the South Korean government for such purposes as issuing passports to Korean residents who registered as South Korean nationals. Under the treaty, this status entitled them to permanent residence. Not surprisingly, from this time on the majority of Korean residents gravitated to the Mindan which could provide practical assistance on a day-to-day level. The Soren retained its emotional tug and its political activism.

Through the late 1960s and early 1970s, the Soren and its allies carried out several successful campaigns to block Diet Bills which would have adversely affected the Korean community. First was a series of Foreigners' School Bills, proposed as a reaction against the expansion of the Soren's ethnic school system. This education system was largely financed by North Korea using North Korean texts. In 1968, a North Korean University was established with the help of a Left-wing prefectural administration in Tokyo.

The proposed Bills sought to suppress these developments by giving the Minister of Education authority to license or close foreign schools, investigate administration and textbooks, and control staff appointments. These moves were opposed not only by a wide range of liberal Left-wing activists but also by leading jurists who invoked the Declaration of Human Rights on parents' rights to determine their children's education. The bills finally failed, despite the control of the Diet by the Liberal Democratic Party which, because it was a coalition of interests rather than a monolithic organization, felt unable to override the substantial opposition of factions within its own ranks.

The next such campaign followed a similar course. It aimed at a series of Bills to amend the Immigration Control Law in order to enforce much more stringent controls over alien nationals in Japan. It is paradoxical that the entire unnaturalized Korean community is subject to this law, since most have been born in Japan and are not immigrants. But this does not seem unnatural to the Japanese who draw no distinction between nationality and ethnicity. From their viewpoint, no Korean or other foreigner can ever become a full Japanese. True Japaneseness can come only through birth.

The moves to tighten controls over the Korean community arose in the tense atmosphere of the late 1960s, when organized opposition to the Vietnam War began, and the opposition was preparing a massive campaign against the renewal of the Security Treaty with the United States scheduled for 1970. The impetus for the proposed Bills arose from anti-war demonstrations involving foreign students. While the original purpose of the legislation was to prohibit such activity, it was soon broadened to include all resident aliens. The range of activities permitted them was to be restricted, and any transgression was subject to prohibition orders and stricter penalties including deportation. But once again a similar alliance of factions succeeded in having the Bills shelved.

Some other battles concerned the Korean community more specifically. One was a law proposed in 1971 on Speculative Game Parlors. At this time, Koreans were operating about 60 percent of the 12,000 parlors in Japan. The aim of the proposed legislation was to exclude operators with criminal records, set a minimum size of business, and transfer authority for closures from local public safety committees to police headquarters. This was defeated by lobbying Japanese business associates. Although the exclusion of those with criminal records might sound reasonable enough, in the Japanese context many Koreans had criminal records as a result of police attitudes of discrimination and harassment for minor or non-existent offenses (alien registration or fingerprinting etc.).

The Law on Businesses involving Moral Considerations introduced in 1984 would have conferred arbitrary powers on public safety committees to investigate and license businesses in the entertainment and hospitality fields thought capable of endangering morals. The Koreans were able to secure only limited amendments to the Bill, despite waging a campaign over 33 prefectures.

The most prominent recent episode involving Korean interests in this type of business was a 1989 media campaign alleging tax evasion and massive contributions to the Socialist party by Korean *pachinko* operators. It is true that some years before this case, Socialist Party mediation had achieved an agreement on taxation between Soren affiliated businesses and the Taxation Office. Political contributions by aliens were, however, illegal and LDP members took up the matter in the Diet, attacking the Soren as a subversive organization and a purveyor of anti-Japanese education. This, as on many such occasions, led to violence against students attending Korean schools.

North Korea has been a bogey exploited by conservatives throughout its history and the occasion of countless harassments to members of the Soren as well as others. The Normalization Treaty of 1965 had recognized the ROK as the sole legitimate government of Korea, and for long afterward re-entry permits to visit North Korea were not available to resident Koreans. Commercial interests, however, finally led to a relaxation of the ban, beginning with a delegation to celebrate Premier Kim Il-sung's sixtieth birthday, in 1972. In 1973, he addressed a business delegation in characteristic style: 'You are not essentially capitalists but have become businessmen as a result of assiduous toil to survive. You may be viewed as patriotic and progressive businessmen working for the sake of the fatherland.' (*O Zai-Nichi Chosenjin Kigyo* 1992)

Soren affiliated business has certainly fulfilled such a role. From the mid-1970s mechanisms were developed for the import and processing of North Korean products and their marketing in Japan and elsewhere. In 1984, the DPRK enacted a Joint Ventures Law, by which it was hoped that Overseas Koreans could play a similar role in their homeland to those of Overseas Chinese and Poles. In response, in 1986 a Joint Venture Research Association was established in Japan. The DPRK promptly established a coordinating Joint Venture Company in Pyongyang. Both parties attended a DPRK light industries fair in Moscow in 1987 and over the next few years, 39 new enterprises were spawned in fields as various as clothing and piano manufacturing, medicinal herb exports, and products based on rare earth and other minerals readily available in North Korea.

These ties led to frequent harassment by Japanese officials. This was most dramatic in 1994 when an international crisis arose over North Korea's reported development of nuclear weapons. Soren members were accused of financing this research and exposing Japan to a nuclear threat. It was proposed that all finance from Japan to Korea be stopped but because of the variety of alternative avenues open to the Soren this was soon deemed impractical. Instead popular hostility against Koreans was vented against students dressed in the conspicuous uniforms of the North Korean oriented schools.

There were over 100 cases of harassment and assault during the months of April-June 1994. A typical assault case occurred on 14 April when a man attacked a 16-year-old female student in Tokyo, cutting her school uniform and injuring her. On 13 May, four Korean boys, all third graders at a Korean junior high school in Tokyo, were assaulted by a group of twenty teenagers. Two of the boys received severe facial injuries. Verbal abuse was even more common with students being told to: 'Go back to Korea' and taunted with 'you make me sick.'

Meanwhile, the end of the Cold War was generating a vastly changed environment for the Soren, both internationally and domestically with the end of the LDP's long monopoly of power in 1993. Internally also the change of generations was bringing new perspectives. Although the intermediate to younger generation was becoming aware of the need to adapt to the new situation, as seen in the 1993 revision of the Soren schools' curriculum, described below, Kim Il-sung's death in July 1994 found the organization ill-prepared for the ensuring uncertainty. The reaction of a teacher vividly expresses the emotional impact of his death:

> Ae-son could not stop crying. She was sad because she felt she had not always fulfilled the duty assigned by the Great Leader. She was sad because she could not bring about the reunification while the Great Leader was alive. She was sad because she had not always been faithful to the Great Leader. She was sad because she did not think North Korea would be all right without the Great Leader. 'Why not sad? We grew up did we not, singing that he was our father and we his children. We learned about him all our school days and I taught my students about him. I do not think one has to be a revolutionary or patriot to be affected by our Great Leader's death. The Great Leader personifies our youth, our memory and nostalgia.' (Ryang 1996)

A factor tending to hinder adaptation to change was the local reflection of the personality cult presented by Han Dok-su's stubborn hold on Soren's chairmanship. In the Fourteenth Congress in the late 1980s, an attempt was made, with the backing of Kim Il-sung's designated successor Jong-il, to replace Han with the vice-chairman Li Jin-gyu, himself quite a senior figure, but this was unsuccessful. Later, a compromise was made by appointing a second-generation junior vice-chairman, but every major decision requires Han's ratification.

Meanwhile, Han maintains what seems to be accepted as an appropriate life-style in a grand residence in an up-market area of Tokyo. A team of security guards watch his home in shifts twenty-four hours a day. Chauffeurs maintain and drive his several luxury cars and bodyguards accompany him whenever he goes out. Housemaids look after his daily life, while others employed in Soren's central headquarters specialize in cooking for him there. These young women are selected Korea University graduates chosen on the basis of 'sound' family background, good academic record, and physical beauty.

Han's daughters have received special treatment. After graduation, they were assigned to relatively undemanding yet highly regarded positions such as Korea University lecturer or researcher. They were given a house in Tokyo when they were married. Even Han's grandchildren's future is assured in both social and economic terms. All this is met by the Soren's budget.

It seems clear that anachronistic factors such as these have eroded the Soren's membership to the point where 78 percent of the un-naturalized Korean population are now said to hold South Korean nationality. The first generation is now described as migrational, retaining nostalgia for South Korea and maintaining family links there even when loyalty is directed towards the North. The second is described as diaspora, more exclusively devoted to the North since the South has not been experienced but merely judged by stereotype; more institutional and less passionate. The third is described as post-diaspora, more individual than state oriented. The individual is therefore more skilled at coping with dual living modes, neatly partitioning organizational and extra-organizational life. This generation tends both to know more about North Korea and to be more critical of it, as 'special permanent residence' eases re-entry to Japan enabling graduation trips for Korea University students and more frequent family visits to repatriates. Travel elsewhere is more common and makes the individual more cosmopolitan and better adjusted to multiplicity.

The Mindan

The secessionists from the Choren who formed the Mindan tended to represent the more prosperous segment of the community. They worked in black market and more legitimate fields but shared no common interests, either material or ideological, except for a general antipathy to Marxism. They remained highly factionalized and lacked the will or capacity for the activism that characterized the Soren. When the Republic of Korea was established, with its mission in Japan, the Mindan was entrusted with processing applications for registration of Koreans as citizens of the ROK, the prerequisite for the issue of passports for overseas travel. Applicants were charged exorbitant fees. Under the 1965 Normalization Treaty, the Mindan gained official status in handling this registration, which by then conferred improved conditions of permanent residence and admission to the national health insurance system. Otherwise, national health insurance for Korean residents was left to the discretion of local government, just as it had been for many years.

The Mindan did participate in some efforts to improve the lot of Koreans. Despite the formal illegality of such contributions, it is generally thought to have furthered its interests by making contributions to the Liberal Democratic and Democratic Socialist Parties. It tried to get South Korean politicians to tone down their anti-Japanese rhetoric so as to minimize the repercussions on the community in Japan.

Like the Soren, the Mindan maintained educational facilities but on a much more limited scale. Activities were mainly restricted to extracurricular classes in Japanese schools or adult education. Despite some financial aid from South Korea, its membership mainly used the Japanese public educational system. Although the majority of the Korean community affiliated with the Mindan used this membership to obtain advantages available to citizens of the ROK, most members view it as an essentially bureaucratic institution.

The associated South Korean Youth League has lobbied for a more activist and socially-oriented role for the Mindan. In the early 1980s, it published a membership survey of opinions and suggestions. The Mindan's functions were described as 26 percent concerned with domicile registration and 56 percent with passports. Its satisfaction rating was given as 40 percent, with 30 percent each dissatisfied or undecided. The general estimate of the organization was that it was essentially bureaucratic, dominated by status seekers or business interests, and more directed to South Korean interests than to the welfare of the community in Japan.

Generational change has brought some re-orientation in the direction of a New Mindan. The name was modified to omit the word 'Residents' (Kyoryu) since this was felt to convey a sense of transience rather than permanence. It has taken a fairly active part in the widely effective agitation for foreign residents' suffrage in local elections, though avoiding the more radical demand for national suffrage as inconsistent with ties to South Korea. Members tend to feel that the reunification of Korea offers the best hope for the future of the Korean community in Japan.

The Mintoren

Given that the Soren and Mindan were predominantly oriented towards the regimes in North and South Korea, social issues affecting the Korean community in Japan tended to receive less attention. As Gerhard Gohl put it in *The Korean Minority in Japan*, they had concentrated on the vertical aspect (North-South confrontation) rather than the horizontal (common social concerns). It was natural that later generations in Japan, more socialized to that society, would wish to move in the opposite direction. The younger generation was better educated and had absorbed a much deeper awareness of human rights issues than their elders, who had grown up under different value systems. The same applied to many of their Japanese contemporaries. The Left-wing moved away from revolutionary to reformist ideals, which in turn gained influence beyond circles necessarily associated with the Left. So by the early 1970s, it was becoming possible for Korean and Japanese activists to combine forces, though not within a rigid framework.

One Japanese activist describes his awakening to the Korean issue:

> It was about seven years ago that I first felt that I had to come to grips with the Korean question as an issue bearing on my own manner of life. It was when I saw a film recording a factual survey on the forced draft of Koreans that I happened to be shown during my judicial training course.
>
> It began with the mines near Nagasaki and the North Kyushu coal fields and went on to explore the realities of the draft labor scene all the way from these places to Hokkaido, on all the noteworthy mines, dams, tunnels, and military installations throughout the country. The survey mainly consisted of oral interviews with first generation residents who had been compulsorily drafted, so that their live testimony was recorded.
>
> The film's contents were shocking. It was simply a matter of press-ganging, enslavement, massacre. I still clearly remember how, on viewing this film, I came to view Japan very differently. Beneath the key installations that have sustained Japan's post-war development—its mines, coal fields, dams, harbors and airports—are buried the corpses of countless Koreans, all unknown!
>
> I felt that as a human being and as a Japanese, I had to share in a task of historical restitution. (Tokoi 1990)

The Mintoren, as its name implies, is not a formal organization but a citizens' movement, each of its campaigns being self-financed on an ad hoc basis. The movement arose from a celebrated lawsuit launched in 1970 against the Hitachi Company on grounds of ethnic discrimination in employment. This became a turning point in the political awakening of the Korean community. It occurred during the period of widespread protest movements in the years around 1970, including movements against oppressive legislative proposals on immigration and education.

The enthusiasm and comradeship generated during this period are recalled by a female Korean student activist of the time, Cha Yuk-cha. (Fukuoka 1991) During her first year of Senior High School, there was practically no teaching, since classes were entirely taken up by debate. 'We set up barricades in the schoolyard. It was terrific! It was delightful! We were free!' In such an atmosphere, she did not need to hide her Korean identity.

At the center of the landmark Hitachi case, which crystallized the social predicament of many Koreans, was a youth named Pak Chong-sok. As was customary, he normally used the Japanese alias Arai Shoji. On graduating from a secondary level commerce course, he obtained work at a small factory of the kind where many Koreans tend to be employed. He soon left because of the management's patronizing attitude. He then noticed a press advertisement for a vacant position at the Hitachi Software Plant at Totsuka near Yokohama. In applying, he used his Japanese name, giving as his permanent domicile his parents' address in Nagoya. In the company examination, out of a field of 32, he qualified for one of the seven vacancies. When he was notified that he had been selected, he was asked to bring his certificate of domicile.

Since he was not a Japanese national, he had only alien registration, not a certificate of domicile. He told the company this by telephone and was informed that his appointment would be withheld until further notice. When he heard nothing, he telephoned again. This time he was told: 'We do not as a rule employ aliens. It is we who have been inconvenienced, rather than you. This would not have happened if you had written the truth. Please resign yourself. Your employment is canceled.'

This treatment is typical of how top-level companies deal with Korean applicants. If their alien status is revealed on application, they are not considered for a job. Up to that time, Koreans had accepted this treatment. Pak, however, determined to take action. At Yokohama Station, he encountered a Japanese student activist demonstrating against the oppressive amendments to the Immigration Control Law, and he approached him for help. The Japanese student recalls:

> I was addressed by a lanky Korean who asked for cooperation in launching a law suit against Hitachi for discrimination in employment. At this I felt two things. The first, quite by reflex, was that we must take it on. The 'Immigration Control Struggle' was then at its peak, and it was self-evident to those in the student movement that we must combat oppression of all sorts against Koreans. The other thing was an indescribable perplexity. I had in a nonchalant way been habitually distributing leaflets about the 'discrimination and oppression suffered everywhere by Koreans' but had never delved into the content of the immigration control system. Perhaps we were overwhelmed by something that we could not quite comprehend. (Kim Il-myon 1978)

Pak felt that he had a case in terms of infringement of the Labor Law. With four students, he formed a group called the 'Committee to Support Pak Chong-sok' and began to gather support for a lawsuit. Neither the Soren nor the Mindan would support him, since Pak's campaign seemed directed at assimilation. He did, however, receive support from semi-assimilated younger Koreans, as well as a broad range of Japanese activists such as teachers, who are widely inclined to social activism, and members of the Burakumin Problem Research Association. New Left people in public bodies, researchers on Korean problems, and other citizens' groups also helped. Besides the prosecution of the lawsuit, the Committee held well-publicized monthly study meetings where, apart from the immediate issues, questions were raised about the nature of the Emperor system and Japan's 'economic aggression in Asia.' A total of 7,800 activists were mobilized and eight regional committees formed. These pressured Hitachi wherever its operations were located throughout the country.

In court, Hitachi maintained that it did not practice ethnic discrimination. It claimed that Pak had been rejected not because he was a Korean but because he had made a false entry in his application (his use of a Japanese alias) and was therefore untrustworthy. To back up its claims, Hitachi conducted a search for Koreans among its staff and found a total of 11 among 80,000 employees. Investigations revealed, however, that local agents of the company had in each case, for their own private reasons, employed them in defiance of company policy and had concealed their identity as Koreans.

When the case became known in South Korea, Hitachi was attacked by the press. Three Christian church bodies led a boycott of Hitachi products. In April 1974, the Committee to Fight Racial Discrimination of the World Council of Churches met in Holland and passed a resolution for a world boycott, as well as contributing a sum of ¥4.5 million to the Committee to Support Pak Chong-sok. The European press was intrigued by the spectacle of a single Korean youth challenging the multinational Hitachi, which soon ceased pressing its case.

After three and a half years of litigation, the court ordered Pak's hiring. He was confirmed as holding due rights under a labor contract and was awarded back pay up to the period of the judgment as well as other compensation.

This campaign and Pak's dramatic legal vindication was the Korean community's greatest triumph. It became a major stimulus for Koreans to demand their rights. Pak reflected on the case: 'If it were not for this case, I would still be leading an unfulfilled and pointless life in some corner around Nagoya [where his parents lived]. I feel as if, in a certain sense, I should offer some thanks to Hitachi for giving me the opportunity to mature to this extent.'

In 1975, a general conference of all the participants to this campaign was held. It was decided to hold such a meeting annually to review developments and devise strategies for current issues. An early success was the securing of Child Allowances from the city of Kawasaki, an important center for Koreans between Tokyo and Yokohama. The success of the Mintoren in Kawasaki prompted the Mindan to take up similar negotiations with the local administration in Osaka, the largest center of Koreans in Japan. This in turn stimulated the organization to take more interest in social issues.

Some major areas where successes were achieved over the following years were in admission to public housing run by local authorities, eligibility of Koreans for scholarships from scholarship societies, employment with the Japan

Telecommunications Corporation, and public employment with local authorities, particularly in the Kansai area. As will be seen in the next section, many of these gains were later extended to a national level as a result of international pressures or diplomacy. It was the Mintoren, however, that accomplished useful pioneering work at the grassroots level.

Many of its aims remain unfulfilled. In 1989, the Mintoren published a proposed Law on Post-war Compensation and Guarantee of Human Rights for Residents of Japan Originating from Former Colonies. This would include an agency to eliminate discrimination in employment for alien residents. It would be comparable with those established under United Nations agreements to secure such rights for women and disabled persons, even though these in practice are often not as effective as might be hoped.

Issues of war compensation have been the subject of court action for a number of years. One notable case is that launched in December 1991 by former comfort women and ex-military and paramilitary servicemen. The official Japanese stand is that all claims by Koreans were settled by the collective payment made to South Korea under the 1965 Normalization Treaty.

Part Two
LEGAL ISSUES

4 The evolution of the Korean community's legal status

The Japanese annexation of Korea was completed in 1910. In the normalization talks attempted by Japan and the DPRK in the early 1990s, the North Koreans laid down as a prerequisite that Japan acknowledge the 'evil and illegal nature of colonialism.' The Japanese maintained that their rule was legitimate according to the international practice of the time and that reparations which may apply between sovereign belligerent states are inapplicable in this case.

In the Western penetration of East Asia from the mid-nineteenth century, the Japanese were realistic enough not to oppose by force the Five-Power unequal treaties imposed upon them. Korea, however, held out longer, earning the epithet of 'the Hermit Kingdom.' The Koreans repulsed two tentative expeditions by the French and Americans and referred others to China on the grounds that China, as Korea's traditional suzerain, was responsible for its foreign relations. But as China itself was reduced to semicolonial status, Korea was finally obliged to enter into diplomatic relations with interested Powers, beginning with Japan after a show of 'gunboat diplomacy.'

In the last decades of the nineteenth century, Japan, Britain, France, Russia, and even China all stirred the Korean pot. A climax came in 1900, however, when Russia, having earlier annexed the maritime provinces of Manchuria as far as the Korean border, took advantage of the 1900 Chinese Boxer Rebellion to occupy the whole of Manchuria and intensify its maneuvers in Korea. The Japanese viewed a foreign controlled Korea as a 'dagger pointed at the heart of Japan,' and Britain was equally alarmed at this major advance by its long-time rival in the Balkans, India's hinterland, and East Asia. The outcome was the Anglo-Japanese alliance, Japan's defeat of Russia, and a free hand for Tokyo in Korea.

The United States also accepted Japan's position in Korea in exchange for Japanese noninterference in the Philippines, where resistance was still being met. In Korea, an important minority party had been organized some years earlier as the Isshinkai or Unity Association. This organization was prepared to collaborate with the Japanese takeover as the only alternative to what they viewed as a completely discredited regime and social order.

The first decade of Japanese rule was a purely military occupation, run by the army and military police, the Kempeitai, who began the expansion of their normal function in the armed forces to one of political suppression, something later extended to wartime Japan. Their main tasks were the putting down of fairly widespread though localized resistance and the wholesale reorganization of Korean society through a land survey and a new system of land-holding. To some extent this followed the reorganization of Japanese land-holding from feudal title to a modern type of ownership, with taxation in cash.

In Korea, all land ownership was regarded as ultimately vested in the monarch and the scholar gentry, the Yangban, who administered the realm and drew revenues corresponding to their functions. The vast peasant majority were illiterate and had no means of asserting their rights effectively against either the Yangban or the new Japanese administration.

The land survey comprised a topographical survey, the assessment of land values for taxation purposes, and the establishment of ownership. The latter was based on documented application for recognition of claims arising out of earlier practices; the peasants were unable to complete the required documentation to prove ownership and were at the mercy of the Yangban who had both literacy and all the records. Land for which there was no satisfactory application became state land and was then sold to Japanese landlords or enterprises. The dispossession of the peasantry that followed was made clear by the 1918 land survey. This showed that 3.3 percent of the agriculturists held 50.4 percent of the cultivated land, 19.6 percent were owner cultivators, 39.3 percent were part owners, part tenants, and the remaining 37.6 percent were landless tenants subject to rents of 60 percent or more of the crop.

Although there is no indication of mass starvation under Japanese rule comparable to the 1.5 million deaths estimated in the Irish famine of the 1840s, dispossession and exploitation exerted pressures for migration. This was at first mainly directed towards the more accessible and sparsely occupied areas of Manchuria and the Maritime Province of Siberia, where Koreans had settled earlier. Migration to Japan had been generally barred up to annexation by a ban on foreign labor in most industries. As a result, the number of Korean residents in Japan in 1909 is given as 790. They were virtually all students.

Even after annexation, when Koreans ceased to be foreign, migration was very slow up to 1916, when the figure reached something over 5,000. Apart from students, who throughout remained a sizable group, most of these were voluntary migrants of the owner-farmer class who could afford to travel, though their occupations in Japan were mainly laboring or peddling. There was, however, already some recruitment by Japanese enterprises, the earliest being Settsu spinning in Osaka, the nucleus of much later growth. Recruitment was much stimulated by World War I with the expansion of Japanese industries to meet shortages created in the economies of Allied countries, the main areas being textiles (which employed mostly women workers), chemical, and coal-mining.

The Korean population in Japan roughly tripled in 1917 and from there on until World War II increased yearly without exception, despite fluctuations in policy and changing economic factors. From the beginning, the great bulk of migration to Japan came from the adjacent southern provinces, as the outlet for the north continued to be the land frontier. Three different sets of figures are reported over the whole period, mainly owing to the mobile nature of Korean labor which was characterized by both frequent shifts around Japan and substantial movement backwards and forwards to Korea. Figures for returnees in most years exceed 50 percent of new entries. The various total estimates are, however, of the same order of magnitude, varying within about 20-30 percent, with closer agreement in the 1930s.

After 1917, some companies opened regular contract offices in Korea, while others relied on local agents, either Japanese or Korean, who could be highly unscrupulous. Many also migrated on their own initiative and a survey in 1927 indicated that 73 percent of migrants had been introduced to prospective employment through relatives or friends. This meant that groups from the same area tended to congregate in a particular locality or industry. Opportunities were certainly better than in Korea, though earnings tended to approximate only 60 percent of those of their Japanese counterparts. A survey in 1929 indicated that 80 percent of Korean residents were manual laborers which, together with their peasant background, gave the community in Japan a lasting uncouth image.

An important turning point was marked by the March First Movement of 1919. This defining event was organized by religious leaders, Christian, Buddhist, and syncretist Heavenly Path adherents, for the very good reason that religious organizations were the only kind allowed at the time. After carefully coordinated preparations, successfully concealed from the Japanese authorities, 33 religious leaders assembled on the appointed day at Pagoda Park in Seoul, where they signed and read aloud a declaration of independence before thousands of demonstrators. Demonstrations and strikes were held throughout the country and by Korean students in Japan.

Reprisals against the movement were savage. They included the obliteration of whole villages thought to be centers of resistance. Many fled to Manchuria and Shanghai where a 'provisional government' was set up.

Japan's extremely hard-line policy towards Korea moderated during the 1920s under the influence of both international and domestic factors. Domestically, Japan was now entering a period of liberalism and pacifism which lasted until the early 1930s, while internationally, the climate associated with the League of Nations and Wilsonian talk of self-determination compelled a measure of conciliation. An Imperial Rescript promised ultimate equality for

Koreans under the Constitution then in force, and a phase of 'cultural administration' was inaugurated. The Kempeitai, whose methods were felt as oppressive even by Japanese residents in Korea, were replaced by a civil police force including some Koreans. The highly arbitrary powers which the Governor-Generals had long enjoyed were reduced and better regulated under the Central Colonial Ministry.

Koreans were appointed to the civil service and included in advisory organs in local administration. This created a class who had some stake in the existing order and divided them from those aspiring to full independence. In colonial policy, as in other fields, the Japanese proved apt students: the lessons of British imperial policies of divide and rule were not lost on them.

This phase brought new hardships for the Korean people, arising from a drive to increase rice production to make the Japanese Empire self-sufficient in this staple food. The drive to self-sufficiency gained urgency following the Japanese Rice Riots of 1918, which were caused by the homeland's rapid population increase and industrialization. As in other colonial empires, the expansion of agricultural production in Korea might have brought improved efficiency to agricultural production, but it did not benefit the local inhabitants. During a fifteen year period, the reclamation of new areas, improved irrigation, and new rice strains produced an overall crop increase of over 20 percent, but this was countered by a fourfold increase in rice shipments to Japan, with the result that rice consumption per head in Korea fell by about one-third. The rationalization of production in the richest areas also led to a loss of land among smallholders and a further wave of migration to Japan.

The large-scale introduction of Korean rice to Japan was eventually reduced after opposition from Japanese rural interests in the early 1930s. Under Depression conditions, imports contributed to a further disastrous lowering of prices. The only Korean elected to the pre-war Imperial Diet, Pak Ch'un-gum, campaigned against restrictions on Korean rice on behalf of Korean interests profiting from the trade, such as landlords and rice dealers.

Korean migration was somewhat restricted from the time of the March First Movement in 1919. Another factor leading the authorities to restrict migrations was the post-war slump, which the authorities feared might contribute to unrest. In 1919, the Government-General introduced a travel certificate system which remained in effect until 1922, though the resident population continued to grow and in that year reached about 60,000.

In 1923, in the chaos following the great Tokyo earthquake which killed 140,000 and left millions homeless, both popular rumor and Japanese officials conjured up images of a combined Leftist and Korean uprising taking advantage of the disorder. A sizable number of Japanese Leftists were seized by the police and Kempeitai and summarily executed. Korean casualties were, however, much greater, since they were more easily identified. Nearly 6,000 were massacred, mainly by vigilante groups. Without the slightest justification, Koreans were rumored to be setting fires, poisoning wells, and committing wholesale violence. The authorities eventually reined in vigilante lawlessness and prosecuted 160 persons, though their sentences were light. About 24,000 Koreans were sheltered in 'reception centers' and many were later employed on reconstruction work in an effort to normalize relations with the Japanese.

Despite this, migration continued. From 1925, a policy of restricting the entry of Korean laborers without formal legal provision was introduced and police at Pusan, the main port of entry, screened migrants. Passage was denied to all who were either not recruited by legitimate agencies, not assured of employment in Japan, or without at least 10 yen in addition to travel costs. Knowledge of Japanese was also essential. Over the next three years about 127,000 denied entries were recorded, though this would include considerable duplication as many people applied more than once. Subsequently, the language requirement was dropped and numbers of denied entries fell markedly, although intended migrants then also had to possess a letter of introduction from their local police office. From 1931, when the Depression and then the Manchurian incident had substantially altered the economic and strategic situation, identification was tightened and the Manchurian alternative encouraged. In that year, however, the resident population was well over 300,000 and continued to increase.

When manhood suffrage for all over 25 was enacted in 1925, Koreans obtained this right, though it was limited by a requirement of one year's continuous residence at one address, and independent means. A concession sometimes allowed Korean voters, as in Tokyo electorates in the general election of 1932, was that those who were not literate enough to write candidates' names in the customary Chinese characters were allowed to use the Korean phonetic script, *Hangul*. Electoral officers were issued instructions on how to read it. This was feasible because, although this script involves numerous complexities in writing Korean, the transcription of names was fairly straightforward.

Koreans could also stand for election at all levels. From the first such candidate in 1929 to the last election in which they could vote in 1942, 99, including Diet member Pak Ch'un-gum, out of 382 candidates were successful; the others being elected to municipal councils. Civil and professional military services were also open to Koreans under the standard examination system. Up to World War II about 1,000 such appointments were made (600 military and 400 or more civil).

There were no changes in the Korean community's legal status up to World War II which proved to be a disaster for the Koreans. When Japan realized that the war with China, which began in 1937, was going to be protracted, the National General Mobilization Law was passed in 1938. This draconian law authorized the labor draft which began to be applied to Korea in 1939 but was intensified from 1942. An official of the National Labor Service Association charged with rounding up Korean labor, often under press-gang conditions, described the process:

> About a year into the war with America, the situation became unfavorable and national general mobilization [in Japan] reached its limits. Labor shortage became acute in the construction of bases, airfields, roads, harbors, and the like. So the Imperial government adopted as a national policy the utilization of the human resources of the Korean peninsula and drafted Koreans by the issue of Cabinet and ministry ordinances. (Yoshida 1983)

The number of draft laborers and military conscripts entering Japan in the first year, 1939, was 38,700 and by the war's end had totaled 990,000, resulting in an overall Korean presence of about 2,378,000. The program also included the Women's Voluntary Service Corps, totaling something like 200,000, of whom a sizable proportion, perhaps 80,000, were diverted to sexual service of the Japanese armed forces as comfort women.

At the end of World War II, the first formal change in Koreans' status was the loss of the franchise. The electoral law was revised just before the first post-war election. This lowered the voting age and extended the franchise to women but at the same time provided that 'voting rights and the right to stand for election are for the time being suspended for all not covered by the [Japanese] domicile registration law.' This was linked to the initial Occupation treatment of Koreans and others similarly placed as 'liberated people' rather than 'enemy nationals.' It was assumed at the time that all Koreans would be repatriated, but when a substantial number declined that option, it was realized that a better definition of their status was needed. Many Koreans had in fact used their status as 'liberated nationals' to defy Japanese laws forcing the police to enlist the aid of the Choren to keep order.

The Occupation authorities therefore ruled that, pending a peace treaty, Koreans should be treated as Japanese nationals for purposes of food rationing, taxation, education, and land transactions. Amid the prevailing economic disorder, the Koreans held a precarious position. Their most common occupations were black marketing in controlled commodities (there were 17,000 black markets at the peak of this activity), illicit spirit distilling, and the collection of scrap metal from bombed factories and dismantled military installations.

The next blow for the Koreans in Japan came with the application 'for the time being' to all of them, as well as to Taiwanese specified by the Home Minister, of the Alien Registration Ordinance of 1947. This was the last Imperial Ordinance promulgated before the new Constitution took effect. The reason for some differentiation among Taiwanese was that some were reluctant to opt for Chinese nationality because of the oppressive rule in Taiwan. A large scale massacre there made Japanese rule look benign by comparison. Unlike the Taiwanese, the Koreans were given no choice in the matter: the main motive for registration was the uneasy security situation arising out of the Cold War. All Koreans were suspect; anyone might be aligned with North Korea and therefore a subversive.

The declared State of Emergency arising out of the schools dispute of 1948 greatly intensified mistrust of Koreans. The long-lived Yoshida administration, under which the Occupation's 'reverse course' and Japan's future role were defined, further intensified surveillance of the Korean community on such pretexts as the search for illegal distilleries or immigrants, or North Korean spies. The Alien Registration Certificate had to be produced at all times when demanded.

Koreans lose Japanese nationality

In 1950, a Nationality Law was enacted under which nationality was automatically acquired only by birth to parents of Japanese nationality. This differs from birth on the country's territory, common among Western countries. Marriage to a Japanese national ceased to be a qualification for nationality. The main qualifications for naturalization were five years continuous residence, good behavior, and the means or ability to make an independent living. Approval was entirely at the discretion of the Justice Ministry and 'good behavior' tended to be interpreted in terms of assimilation to Japanese social expectations. At this stage, the Koreans were not directly affected by the law since they had not definitively lost Japanese nationality, pending the Peace Treaty.

Although the Peace Treaty when concluded only involved the Western powers (excluding the Eastern bloc and both Chinas), it included a definitive relinquishment to any claim to Korea. When it took effect in 1952, however, a Notification from the Civil Affairs Bureau of the Justice Ministry announced that, in accordance with Japan's relinquishing of sovereignty over Korea and Taiwan, residents originating from those areas had lost Japanese nationality, and if they wished to acquire it they would need to apply for it on the same basis as any other resident aliens. They would not even have the advantages extended to the former Japanese nationals who had lost Japanese nationality for any reason, such as marriage, and wished to regain it.

There can be little doubt that by depriving the Koreans of their Japanese nationality, Japan acted illegally, immorally, and unwisely. Japan's American drafted Constitution states that nationality is to be determined by law, rather than administrative decision. Secondly, the usual international practice allows individual choice of nationality when territorial changes occur (e.g., Austrians in post-war Germany were given a choice of nationality). In this case, however, Japanese officials took the power of choice away from the individual. It

51

was also irrational to make no distinction between other aliens entering Japan with foreign nationality, and former colonial subjects who had come there, often forcibly drafted, as Japanese nationals.

During 1952 a number of Koreans applied for naturalization. Those who applied were in public employment and needed Japanese nationality to retain their jobs. A total of 233 such applications were granted during that year, and numbers gradually increased. Some other early cases were former police or Kempeitai who had served in Korea and, fearing for their lives after defeat, had taken refuge in Japan. Others were disillusioned by dissension within the Korean community itself.

Those who did not apply for naturalization were the vast majority and came under the jurisdiction of the Immigration Control Law, enacted to complement the Nationality Law. Since the Korean community had no passports and Japan had no diplomatic relations with either of the Korean states, which were in any case still at war with each other, a special category had to be provided for them. This was done under Law 126 of 1952, which allowed indefinite residence to all who had lived continuously in Japan since before the formal surrender on 2 September 1945, together with children born to them since, pending an agreement with the ROK on their final status. This was a pro tem arrangement not amounting to permanent residence, since the usual range of grounds for deportation still applied. In practice, deportation only applied to cases of serious felonies or failure to register. Koreans who had broken their post-war stay in Japan, or who had arrived since, lacked even this measure of security. They were subject to ordinary immigration procedures.

The fingerprinting requirement

The most demeaning aspect of the Alien Registration Law and one which provoked many years of confrontation was the fingerprinting requirement. The motives behind it went back both to Japanese practice with Chinese employees of the South Manchurian Railway and to the United States' practice of fingerprinting alien nationals during the Second World War. It was designed to combat subversion in the case of any revived conflict in Korea and to prevent illegal trade in registration certificates. Despite these arguments, the Japanese authorities hesitated. Fingerprinting was associated with criminal proceedings. Enforcement was delayed three times after this law's 1952 enactment until 1955. No renewals of alien registration were due that year and therefore authorities felt they could avoid large-scale protest.

From 1949, with the revival and rationalization of the Japanese economy, the economic position of the Korean community tended to deteriorate still further. Black marketeering and other marginal means of survival disappeared. In mining, where they had occupied a major part of the workforce from the forced draft period, Koreans were replaced by demobilized Japanese. As a result of this policy, the number of Koreans engaged in mining fell from 135,751 in 1945 to only 53 by 1952. (Kang 1989)

Koreans were also initially excluded from the public welfare system, where they were treated as ineligible foreign nationals. Soon after the Korean War began, however, a Notification from the Welfare Ministry extended the scope of the Livelihood Protection Law to former Japanese nationals who had not yet been formally divested of this nationality—but as a humanitarian gesture rather than a right. This policy was continued after the Peace Treaty and meant that administrative rulings in this field could not be questioned or contested.

Statistics reflect the Koreans' economic position. In 1951, when recipients of assistance under this law amounted to 2.4 percent of the total Japanese population, 9.9 percent of alien residents, almost entirely Koreans, were on public welfare. A peak was reached in 1955, when 21.4 percent of all Koreans were receiving public welfare as against 2.2 percent for the whole population. In 1956, procedures were tightened. There was a general survey of welfare assistance for aliens, and as a result the percentage of Koreans on welfare in 1957 dropped to 12.7 percent, still far higher than for the Japanese population. Statistics for October 1952 show 64.4 percent of Koreans, including both sexes, as 'unemployed' or 'no occupation' and only 27.1 percent in 13 classes of legitimate occupations. The boom in the economy since 1960 reduced the percentage of Koreans and Japanese on welfare, but throughout the whole post-war period, the Korean figure has remained far above the national average.

The number of destitute Koreans in the midst of Japan's booming economy was greater than indicated by these statistics. Some may have lacked information, and an unknown number were prevented by pride from falling back on welfare. In one case, a woman forced to rely on welfare when her husband entered hospital with tuberculosis later paid back what she had received from the state when the family finances were restored. In a situation where widespread poverty led to the Koreans both being despised by the Japanese majority and feeling inferior themselves, she used this gesture to impress on her daughter that being a Korean need be no cause for dishonor. (Fukuoka 1991)

There was no material change in the Koreans' status until the long deadlock with the Rhee regime gave way to compromise in the 1965 Normalization Treaty with the ROK. This consisted of a Basic Treaty covering interstate relations, with four supplementary agreements including a definition of the legal and welfare status of Korean residents in Japan. The latter were not consulted. Their organizations such as the Mindan were weak, and most other organizations were either apolitical or, under Soren influence, opposed the treaty on the grounds that it would intensify the division of Korea. The Prime Minister of South Korea even suggested that the best solution was for all to naturalize. Repatriation to South Korea was never welcome, as Koreans from

Japan were often thought likely to be infected by Marxism or in some other way inclined to disturb the political order.

The 1965 Normalization Treaty

The negotiations over the 1965 Treaty, as well as the whole story of the 1945-65 period, show that the Korean residents in Japan live in a legal, cultural, and psychological limbo: too Korean for Japan to accept but also too Japanese for South Korea even to contemplate taking them back.

The Koreans in Japan were entirely neglected in the matter of compensation to Korea or Koreans arising from colonization and war. Even those who were injured while serving in the Japanese military, the victims of forced labor, bombing, or other military actions were equally neglected. Reparations in the usual sense were not regarded as applicable, since Japan had not been at war with South Korea. It was, however, recognized that valid claims would exist for individuals in such areas as unpaid wages, savings held in Japan, or damages which could be documented. In most cases, however, documentation was unavailable because of the widespread destruction resulting from the Pacific and Korean wars, as well as considerable deliberate destruction of records by Japanese authorities at the end of the war. Finally, the Choren, soon after the War, had already collected the funds due on many such claims, and had used the money for its own purposes.

Meanwhile, the Park regime in the ROK was in dire need of economic aid from the now prosperous Japan. It agreed to accept a collective settlement of all such claims, leaving the ROK government with responsibility to distribute compensation to individuals whose cases could be established. In the event, only a small proportion was distributed, mainly to the families of military and paramilitary war dead and in any case could only apply to Koreans resident in South Korea. This issue was only revived many years later, in late 1980s, when the Cold War was fading and settlements made under its influence could be challenged, though to date with no success. The Japanese funds provided under the treaty were described as comprising an Independence Congratulation Fund, rather than compensation, and consisted of US$300 million in grants and US$200 million in soft loans.

The preamble to the treaty read in part:

> In consideration of the fact that these nationals of the Republic of Korea have resided for many years in Japan and have come to bear a special relationship with Japanese society, it will contribute to the advancement of friendly relations between our two countries and peoples if those Korean nationals are enabled to achieve a stable livelihood within the framework of Japanese society.

54

There is no hint here of any moral responsibility on Japan's part towards a community that was originally created by Japan's pre-war colonial policies including forced labor and wartime draft. Seoul did not protest these euphemisms partly because of the mixed feelings the Seoul government had towards the Koreans in Japan but mainly because of the benefits it anticipated through cooperation with Japan.

The most important provision of the Treaty was permission for permanent residence for all registered citizens of the ROK who had lived continuously in Japan from before 15 August 1945, the date of the Emperor's announcement of surrender. They had to apply by 17 January 1971. Also included were their children born by this date, so long as they had lived continuously in Japan, and their own children, born subsequently. Permanent residence was only offered to three generations, but it was agreed that, if the ROK were to request it, further consultations on the status of subsequent generations would be held in 1991, 25 years after the date of the Treaty. Citizenship was not offered under the Treaty.

The Japanese were unwilling to accept the prospect of a permanent unassimilated minority. They hoped that by 1991 either naturalization or repatriation might have eliminated the problem. Pluralism on the Western model was simply inconceivable. (Nor would pluralism be acceptable to the Korean government or indeed most Asian countries.)

The grounds for deportation for permanent residents under the Treaty were restricted to those sentenced to seven years or more imprisonment, three years or more for violation of narcotics control laws, or any case of crime against the head of a foreign state or diplomatic envoy. Under the terms of the treaty, South Korea was obliged to accept all deportees, even those affiliated to the North for whom deportation was often worse than a death sentence. This is a major reduction of grounds as compared with those for most alien residents. But are any grounds for deportation appropriate for the long settled Korean community, over and above any penalty imposed within Japan? In contrast, however, to the other aliens living in Japan of their own free will, Koreans had come there as a result of Japanese actions of one sort or another whether migrating in search of work or as forced labor, forced to serve as 'comfort women,' or been conscripts of other types. Owing to Japanese suppression of Koreans' education system, they had largely lost their ancestral language and culture, so that quite apart from the pain involved in a family breakup and the loss of livelihood in Japan, adjustment to life in Korea would involve extreme hardship.

Another provision of the Treaty was Japanese agreement to expedite procedures for granting 'general permanent residence' for Koreans who had not lived continuously in Japan for the required period and were disqualified under Law 126 or the Treaty. This was defined in 1969. Holders of this status were not entitled to the welfare measures granted under the Treaty, comprising full entitlement under the Livelihood Protection Law (though others continued to receive it as a 'humanitarian measure') and National Health Insurance, otherwise left to the discretion of local authorities. South Korean demands for Koreans' inclusion in the National Pension system were parried on the grounds that this involved a long-term joint insurance framework. The Japanese agreed to study the matter of admission to public housing, adding that some local authorities already allowed this. They also guaranteed to continue to admit Korean pupils to the public education system on the same basis as Japanese nationals but would continue to treat ethnic schools as 'miscellaneous schools' which did not qualify for access to advanced public education.

In respect to access to occupations, the legal, medical, and nursing professions were described as open to all with the necessary qualifications. In some of these areas, however, problems in attaining such qualifications persisted for many years mainly because of discrimination and the consequent disadvantages which Koreans suffered in the education system.

Japan agreed to note South Korea's request for affiliated credit unions to obtain finance under the Housing Finance Corporation Law, though a more general request to allow their handling of finance from finance corporations was regarded as excessively complex.

Concerns regarding public housing were settled with the next major development bearing on the rights of permanent alien residents, namely the ratification in 1979 of the International Covenant on Human Rights. Although no actual legislative changes were made, Notifications from the Construction and Finance Ministries soon afterwards removed the nationality qualifications from the Public Housing and the Housing Finance Corporation Laws.

Asked about the broader implications of this ratification, Prime Minister Ohira stated that public employment for alien nationals was only excluded in the case of 'positions involving the exercise of public authority or the formation of government policy.' Local authorities, he said, were free to interpret this as seemed appropriate. This formula derived from a guideline issued by the Ministry of Home Affairs in 1973. Since, however, many local authorities were by then under progressive administrations, some took advantage of a broader interpretation to admit Koreans to public employment. This included some teaching positions, despite the Education Ministry's discouraging this practice by local school boards not under its direct formal control.

Advances in the 1980s

Substantial legislative improvements occurred in 1981 when Japan ratified the Treaty on the Status of Refugees. This became a major international issue because of the mass exodus of Boat People from Vietnam. Japan could not credibly remain aloof. The Treaty committed signatories to amend appropriately any domestic legislation conflicting with it. Recognized refugees had to be accorded the same treatment as nationals in social security provisions. The abolition of the nationality requirement from social security legislation meant that Korean residents also became eligible.

The Welfare Ministry objected to extending the National Pension system, but this was overcome by replacing the Minister with a former Foreign Minister who better understood the situation and the measure was passed the following year. Transitional arrangements for Koreans were, however, unsatisfactory since 25 years' contribution before the age of 60 was required, thus excluding those over 35. This requirement was later altered to a pro rata pension which still disadvantaged older residents, even though they had been paying normal taxes throughout their working lives.

Child allowances became available in 1982 and the National Health Insurance system became fully applicable to Koreans in 1986. Provisions for permanent residence were also widened. Koreans not registered as ROK nationals through the Mindan, who were still subject to the provisional Law 126 of 1952, were allowed five years to apply for a Concessional Permanent Residence status. Most did so. This status was, however, still inferior to that conferred by the ROK treaty, since normal provisions for deportation applied, although they were little enforced.

Revision in 1984 of the nationality Law arose from ratification of the Convention on the Elimination of all Forms of Discrimination against Women. It provided that Japanese nationality could now be acquired from either parent, allowing a final choice by the age of 22. This decision had to be accepted by the Japanese authorities, thus the individual, rather than the state, had control of the choice. These circumstances tend to favor a prevailing trend to Japanese nationality in the ethnic Korean community. If the mother only is Japanese, the child would first be registered under her domicile for practical reasons, meaning the child has provisional Japanese nationality. Korean nationality could then only be obtained through renouncing Japanese nationality, which in turn would leave an uncertain status regarding permanent residence. By 1989, moreover, 80 percent of Korean marriages were mixed (Welfare Ministry statistics show a majority of mixed marriages from 1976), reflecting a steady drift towards assimilation encouraged by the scattered nature of the Korean community and the divisions within it.

A transitional provision allowed minors with Japanese mothers to acquire Japanese nationality by applying within three years of the 1984 passage of this Law. The following years showed the first drop recorded in the number of Koreans with alien registration beginning with a decline from 687,135 in 1984 to 683,313 in 1985. Naturalization rose from 4,608 to 5,040 and generally maintained this level.

The long-term survival of an identifiable Korean minority seems to depend, as earlier suggested, on maintaining cultural identity, together with Japanese acceptance of a distinction between nationality and ethnicity in a pluralist society. One hint of such a possibility lies in an amendment to the Domicile Registration Law, concurrent with that of the Nationality Law, allowing a child obtaining Japanese nationality to use a Korean surname. This also opened the way to a wider acceptance of naturalization under non-Japanese names, making a symbolic breach in the traditional insistence on assimilation. Another factor in the possible preservation of Korean cultural identity is a general willingness among Japanese wives to accept this.

The following case seems not exceptional:

> Byong-on told me that his Japanese wife had been learning Korean for four years now in the local Soren branch and speaks it much better than himself; he added that she insisted that their son speak Korean to her at home. She can be regarded as a new type of Japanese woman. She is learning Korean not just to follow her husband's need but to surpass it by outmaneuvering Byong-on. She was under no obligation to learn Korean but she opted for it. Perhaps she had her own concern about her mother-in-law as well. He added, 'It embarrasses me, because I hardly remember anything from school except for *widaehan suryongnim* (the Great Leader) and *uri choguk* (our fatherland).' (Ryang 1966)

The 1990s

A move which could improve the lot of many in the Korean community in Japan was a renewed attempt, beginning in 1990, at normalization of relations of Japan with the DPRK. This was prompted by various factors arising out of the end of the Cold War, such as North Korea's growing isolation and the need to diversify economic relations and Japan's need for greater flexibility in dealing with the shifting situation in East Asia. Both Japan and North Korea were concerned about growing Chinese influence in South Korea through economic relations.

A beginning was made in September 1990 by a Joint Liberal Democratic Party and Japanese Socialist Party delegation to the Korean Workers Party. This produced a three-party declaration in which it was stated that Japan should 'fully and officially apologize and compensate' North Korea for 'the enormous misfortunes and misery imposed on the Korean people for 36 years and the losses inflicted on the Korean people in the ensuing 45 years.' After clearing this with the South Korean government, which itself was in a phase of optimism on possible Korean unification, the Japanese began formal negotiations in January. After two meetings in Pyongyang and Tokyo, the venue was shifted to Beijing for ease of communications.

The Japanese immediately ruled out any question of compensation for the post-war period and the North Koreans soon ceased to press this issue. Regarding compensation for the colonial period, the Japanese insisted on the documentation of claims, as they had initially with South Korea. This is, of course, totally impracticable. Some data held in Japan on such issues as the labor draft and comfort women had been unearthed and published under pressure from South Korea and activists in Japan. The North Koreans pressed for such investigations to continue as an aid to clarifying the compensation issue. A partial precedent for compensation to individuals had been set by Japan's agreement, again under South Korean pressure, to compensate Korean victims of the atomic bomb attacks. A foundation, with funds of ¥4 billion, had been formed to assist them following President Roh's visit to Japan in 1990.

The North Korean demand for an apology for colonization was problematic, since this had not been included in the Normalization Treaty with South Korea and Japan was committed to avoiding any disadvantage for South Korea. Other issues raised were the rights of Koreans in Japan not affiliated to South Korea, who in the absence of diplomatic relations were virtually stateless, and for Japanese women married to residents of North Korea permission to visit Japan. There were estimated to be about 1,800 of these, mainly wives of repatriates.

Further improvement of the situation of non-Mindan affiliated Koreans, then numbering slightly under half the total, incidentally arose as a by-product of the South's Normalization Treaty of 1965. A provision held that the status of later generations could be reviewed by 1991, if the ROK so requested. A number of talks were held in the lead-up to this date, extending to all areas of concern. They were summarized in a Memoire issued in January 1991 by Prime Minister Kaifu on a visit to South Korea. The form was not as directly binding as a Treaty, but amounted to a statement of intent subsequently incorporated in legislation.

The Memoire covered five main areas as follows:

1. *Immigration control:* Procedures for permanent residence would be simplified and clearly defined. Grounds for deportation would be limited to serious offenses involving insurrection, foreign invasion, or the national interest in international or diplomatic relations. The time limit for a re-entry permit would be extended to a maximum of five years (previously one year).

2. *Alien registration:* Fingerprinting would be replaced by other forms of identification. Efforts would be made for a more flexible approach to the requirement to carry the Alien Registration Card.

3. *Education:* Appreciating the wish of the Korean community to maintain its language, ethnic tradition, and culture, the Japanese government would exercise care that no hindrance arose to the continued teaching of Korean language and culture in extracurricular courses conducted at the discretion of local authorities. In order to ensure educational opportunities equal to Japanese nationals, guardians would be issued with course guides on a nationwide basis.

4. *Appointment as teachers in public schools:* Prefectural authorities would be directed to authorize examination for general teaching appointment on the same basis as for Japanese. Care would be exercised to ensure stability of status and treatment, having regard to reasonable distinctions arising from difference of nationality in appointment to public office.

5. *Appointment to local public office:* Local public bodies would be directed to endeavor to broaden opportunities for appointment, having regard to reasonable distinctions arising from difference of nationality in appointment to public office.

The ROK government expressed support for Korean suffrage in local elections, but the Japanese made no commitment. This is an issue gaining importance and support as essential to any further improvement in the Koreans' social situation.

On Prime Minister Kaifu's return to Japan, he delivered a message to the nation on the status of the Korean community, the first of this kind. It included the following statement:

> Korean residents of Japan who, through special historical circumstances, have come to share social life with us, have suffered varied and repeated hardships arising from these circumstances and are in need of a stable status and treatment in Japanese society. . . . I consider it most important that they be enabled to lead a life as stable as possible within Japan's social order . . . . The policies announced for fundamental measures in several fields will be faithfully implemented. . . . In undertaking the future development of Japanese society from a world perspective, I believe we must reflect together and live together as members of the same society with these residents of our country . . . . I profoundly hope that we can further deepen our understanding and concern for the situation of Koreans and other foreign nationals having a similar historical background, in the setting of everyday life, in the workplace, or local society. (*Min Zai-Nichi Kankokujin* 1994)

The measures enacted certainly improved matters in a number of respects, though problems remained. Law 71 of 1991 defined the status under Immigration Control of all who had lost Japanese nationality under the Peace Treaty and had lived in Japan since before 2 September 1945. The three categories of permanent residence by treaty, concessional permanent residence, and residence under Law 126 were unified as Special Permanent Residence, which also now applied to future generations. Grounds for deportation were restricted as promised and the limit for re-entry extended to five years.

The following account indicates the effect of these changes on the personal level for a Soren affiliate:

The attitude of the bureaucrats of the Immigration Control Bureau have sufficiently improved. In the mid-1980s whenever I applied for a re-entry permit, I would have to wait for three to four hours, as the office was always under-staffed; the officials would treat me like a criminal, staring and yelling at me all the time in an intimidating fashion. On one occasion I was explicitly told by an official that the re-entry permit was granted solely by the generosity of the Japanese government and I should not demand it as my right; he said, 'You Koreans always take things for granted!' In those days it was a norm for the officials to bully Koreans whenever there was a chance to do so; it happened so regularly that I used to conclude that they were so trained. Only some years later, in 1992, when I showed my alien registration card with special permanent residence, I was not even questioned and a multiple entry permit valid for four years was immediately issued. Now the officials are generally polite and quite all right to deal with. (Ryang 1996)

Law 66 of 1992 abolished fingerprinting for both special and general permanent residents. Penalties for infringement of the Alien Registration Law in regard to address, name, nationality, occupation, status, and duration of residence and nature and location of place of work, which previously could carry a custodial sentence, were limited to a fine of not more than ¥200,000. Instead of fingerprinting, a photograph, signature, and family particulars were required, with a penalty for refusing to sign set at a maximum of one year's imprisonment or a ¥200,000 fine. The photograph had to be of passport format and the signature in the same style as that in the passport, if held. The requirement to carry the Alien Registration Card at all times remained. An important ground for dissatisfaction was the government's retention of all existing fingerprint records.

The nationality requirement was abolished for the examination for appointment as a teacher in the public system, but a distinction from Japanese nationals was preserved by classifying alien nationals as 'full time lecturers' rather than by the normal term for teachers. This was done under the formula mentioned earlier on 'public authority' and 'government policy.' All teaching duties with attendant employment conditions were open to full-time lecturers, but they were ineligible for administrative appointment or promotion. Koreans reacted to these stipulations as yet another humiliation.

Some local authorities, mainly in Osaka and Tokyo, had already, prior to this ruling, appointed Koreans to the full 'teacher' positions. These teachers were allowed to retain this status, but all new appointments had to be that of a 'full-time lecturer.' Agreement had been reached with the ROK to hold ministerial level meetings yearly on resident Korean issues, and the South Koreans subsequently raised this issue but without success.

The attainment of suffrage, at least at the local level, for alien permanent residents has been described as 'the last hurdle' in the campaign to secure full rights. This would clearly define Koreans as full members of the Japanese community. The right to stand for an election would carry the possibility of serving on local government committees, such as welfare and education. This in turn would serve to break down the restriction to public office implied in the 'public authority' formula.

To personalize the issues, I will round off this sketch of legal development with a personal account. This is one of a number of autobiographical reminiscences by young Korean women collected in a book entitled *In Search of My True Self*. (Fukuoka 1991) The account by Kang Sun-ja, formally known by her Japanese name Kyomoto Junko, is representative of those more conscious of their ethnicity.

Sun-ja was aged 40 when interviewed in 1990. She was born in Tokyo to a Korean who had been brought to Japan by his parents in his first year of life. She had attended a Japanese primary school for the first four years under her Japanese name. During that time, she loathed the fact that she was Korean. On being transferred to an ethnic school after her fifth year, however, she came to joyfully accept her heritage and developed a cheerful and vivacious disposition. At the time of her interview, she was working for a business association affiliated to the Soren, as well as teaching Korean to both Koreans and Japanese.

Sun-ja remembers her grandfather, who worked first as a stevedore and later as a scrap metal dealer, as an 'extremely gentlemanly looking figure, wearing a Western-style suit and shiny shoes.' Her father, after graduating from the old-style secondary school, continued in the scrap metal business. He used his Korean name socially, but a Japanese alias in business. He was of serious disposition, neither drinking nor smoking.

Her mother, who was brought to Japan at the age of seven, never attended school and married Sun-ja's father when they were both teenagers. She then helped in his business. Most of Sun-ja's older relatives, although originating from southern Korea like almost all in Japan, repatriated to North Korea during the major program organized by the Soren after 1959. Her father and his family, six daughters and one son, would have accompanied them but, as an aunt had acquired South Korean nationality through marriage, her father was instructed by his father to remain in Japan and look after her interests.

Sun-ja became aware of not being Japanese about the time she moved up from kindergarten to primary school. Clues were her grandparents' conversation in Korean and her mother's wearing of Korean costume when out visiting. Her school report for her first year described her as 'very lively and expressing herself well.' By the third year, however, this had become 'for some reason tends to be downcast.' This was when she was being most bullied at school.

62

There were other Koreans in her class. It was at this age that other children came to be conscious of Koreans and to whisper about who was Korean. Other Korean children tried to deflect bullying from themselves by exposing Sun-ja as Korean. Former friends turned on her. They would say 'Koreans drink too much and go to sleep by the road' or 'they do robberies.' They were, in fact, blamed for every kind of trouble.

Sun-ja asked her teacher to protect her from the bullies. Instead, the teacher too discriminated against her, picking her out for a scolding even when the whole class was in uproar. In her third year, one boy even used extortion. He ordered her to bring him some iron, and she took a bucket to him. He accompanied her to an iron dealer and sold it to him, pocketing the proceeds. Sun-ja's mother had become suspicious and followed them, so realizing for the first time that her daughter was being bullied.

In her fourth year, the teacher was much better. He let it be known that no bullying of Korean children would be tolerated. This teacher even gave the Koreans some special teaching after hours, telling them how their parents came to Japan and suggesting that they might be better off in an ethnic school which would have belonged to the Soren system. Such a teacher may well have been a Left-wing sympathizer, something fairly common in the teaching profession.

Sun-ja's father was very ethnically conscious and would have sent her to a Korean school. Since, however, the nearest was rather far away, he had planned to leave this until secondary school. But by now he was inclined to follow the teacher's suggestion. Sun-ja was violently opposed. The bullying had made her hate being a Korean. At night she longed to wake up Japanese. Her next younger sister told her that when she went to a Korean school, she would have to use the Korean form of her name. Sun-ja refused to learn her Korean name until she entered the ethnic school. After school, she claimed to have forgotten it again.

In her new school, however, she felt relieved and liberated at being surrounded entirely by Koreans. Suddenly it seemed absurd that she had ever regretted being Korean. She felt as if a fog had cleared and reverted to her original lively disposition. She was given every assistance in the language and spoke Korean fluently by her sixth year. (Presumably with the limited vocabulary and range of expression used in the school system. See Ryang 1996 for the limitations of Korean language teaching.)

Sun-ja now feels grateful to the teacher who encouraged her to change schools. 'What I am now, I owe to that teacher.' The manners and customs of a people, she believes, can only be internalized when learned in the company of compatriots. 'The language is the nation. You can't understand your people if you don't know the language.' (This of course marks a clear distinction from Mindan affiliates who study Korean, if at all, in part-time or extra-curricular courses.)

It was from about Sun-ja's time, in the early 1960s, that female students began to wear Korean costume (*chima-chogori* = skirt and top) when attending ethnic schools. During her first secondary year, there was a choice between Korean costume and the sailor blouse worn by Japanese schoolgirls. In her second year, the school authorities conducted a campaign for all girls to wear Korean costumes. This of course made her and her friends conspicuous and an easy target for Japanese bullies.

> When we were going to school we would often run into Japanese school children and it was scary. When they came near us, wearing their school uniforms, we would lower our gaze. Some would call out to us. Sometimes on the Loop Line [in Tokyo] they would call out to us in Korean, something like '*cha mashiro, kaja*' (let's go and have tea). It was scary!

On graduating from Korean senior secondary school, Sun-ja attended a bookkeeping school for a year, using the Japanese pronunciation of her Korean name, which became Kyo Junko. She found that if she concealed her name no one questioned her. She still retains friends from that time. When staff recruiters visited the school, although she realized there was no prospect for Koreans in Japanese business, she tested the situation by applying under her real name. All three attempts were futile and she was told: 'our policy is not to employ aliens.' 'By aliens, they mean Koreans,' she comments.

Until the age of 27, Sun-ja helped with the family business. Then her father was asked to allow her to work at a Soren affiliated business association, where she handled tax matters. This involved consultation with businessmen on their taxation returns and other problems. Her office was also consulted by Mindan-affiliated businessmen: 'After all, underneath, we are all one nation.'

She remained unmarried.

> I suppose it happened not to be my fate. I had one *miai* (interview or introduction for possible marriage) but I then developed a phobia about them. It was a nasty experience, having proposals flooding in regardless of my wishes. Korean parents think that, if a *miai* goes well, you have to marry at once—in a matter of two or three months. They were surprised that I was not inclined that way. Besides, the world of Koreans is so narrow. I thought it best to marry someone of the same nation but, although various inquiries seem to have been made, men from Cheju Island or Cholla Province were ruled out by my parents. [These are in the southwest and traditionally despised by those from the southeast, as the Kangs were]. Besides, the same lineage [of Kangs] was not allowed, so no one was left. (Marriage is, however, allowed between people of the same surname.)

From about the age of 20, Sun-ja has been teaching Korean at a local government youth center school. She obtained pupils by visiting individual homes where the children attended Japanese schools, suggesting they also learn Korean. She also later took up adult classes.

These adult classes in the Culture Center where she teaches are attended by both Japanese and ethnic Koreans. The latter usually come with Japanese aliases, but on identifying them she suggests they use their Korean names. She herself ceased using her alias when she began to teach. Previously, she had continued to use her alias Kyomoto with more casual acquaintances to avoid complex explanations about her background. But her contacts with Japanese and Koreans of other backgrounds have given her a broader outlook than the stricter Soren affiliates.

Regarding the current campaign for local suffrage, however, Sun-ja maintains the Soren line that, 'although she feels left out of things at election time,' Japan is not their country and that the best compensation for the taxes paid by Koreans would be to return them to the ethnic education system.

Although the legal position of Koreans in Japan has improved in many important ways in recent decades, social acceptance is another matter as Sun-ja's case makes clear. The essential humanity of Koreans and other minorities continues to be resisted, whatever the legal advances. In Japan, the concept of Korean Japanese, unlike Polish Americans or even Korean Americans, remains an alien idea. Perhaps no single issue illustrates Japan's difficulty with the idea of pluralism more than the question of names.

5 Names

What's in a name? A great deal. For Koreans, name usage is an intensely emotional matter. Names are not merely a matter of labeling for the sake of practical convenience. In countries developed mainly by free migration, as in North America or Australia, there is little concern whether immigrants retain their original names or change them. For the Koreans in Japan, however, the circumstances could hardly be more different. Certain complexities peculiar to East Asian languages and disparate social traditions, but more particularly the historical circumstances of colonization and largely forced migration, load the subject with an enormous range of symbolic associations. These are intensified by the complex experience of growing up in the Korean community. Some case studies will dramatize just how psychologically disturbing the stripping of Korean names can be to those living in Japan.

Yumi Lee has included information on this issue in her autobiography:

> In my junior high, there were no Korean family names such as Lee, Park and Kim, which would have been obvious. But in my last year of junior high I was told by my teacher that I needed to use my real name for the senior high entrance exam. My teacher called other students individually and secretly. They must have been the Japan born Koreans. I started to associate my Koreanness with something to hide. A negative image of myself was implanted in my mind.
>
> On graduation day, each student was called and handed the diploma at the ceremony. This is the day when we feel a mixed feeling of joy and sadness at separating from friends. When I received my diploma, I choked. I saw two names written side by side. One was my real name, Yumi Lee. The other was Yumi Uno, in parenthesis. An unknown burden was put on my shoulder. I put my diploma away immediately in a case before anyone could see it, and hurried home. It made me feel like a

criminal. My friends were showing their diplomas to each other and talking about junior high days.

Three years later on the day of graduation from senior high school, I experienced the same depression and went home in a hurry. Not being a Japanese generated a feeling like guilt feeling.

I have another bitter memory concerning my name. On the day of the entrance exam to senior high, we had to bring the exam registration card to the venue. My name was written as Yumi Lee. I was tense, and determined that it was not to be seen by anyone. To enter a public high school, we had to sit an exam on seven different subjects, which took all day. I had double pressure: to pass the exam and to hide my name on the card.

That morning students were gathered in the school playground. We were chatting with friends to relieve the tension. A supervisor who happened to be in my group said: 'Do you all have your exam registration cards? Show them to me to make sure.' I thought this was the end of the world. I prayed: 'God, help me. I can't show my card in front of everyone.' I have never asked help from God as desperately as this since I was born. The supervisor started to check the cards individually. He was getting nearer and nearer. I cried again to God in my mind. My prayer worked! I don't know why, but he left just before he got to me. How relieved I was!

When everyone was seated for the exam to start, students were told to place their exam registration cards on the upper right hand side of the desk so that they would be easy to check. I placed my pencil case on my card, just in case. As we had exams on seven different subjects, we had breaks in between. I was all tensed up worrying if anyone would see my card.

When I think back to that day, if anyone had known I was Yumi Lee, not Yumi Uno, he or she would not have known how to deal with it. I myself did not fully understand its significance. In short, I was in a position where I had to hide something that I myself did not really understand. It was as if I had an unknown identity. I certainly did not have an identity as a Korean. I was afraid because I did not know who I was; I was afraid because if someone knew that I was different from the others, I would have felt terrible.

The day the names of those who had passed the exam for the high school were presented on a huge board at the entrance to the school, I was again worried. What if I was listed as Yumi Lee? I was happy to find I had passed the exam but, more than anything else, I was relieved to find my name listed as Yumi Uno. If it were written Lee, it would, I felt, have been a big scandal.

Yumi Lee's 'coming out' began following her first visit to Korea. It was foreshadowed earlier at a surprise encounter at the preparatory meeting at the Mindan's Kyoto office.

When I went to the meeting, someone called my name: 'Yumi!' I was pleasantly surprised. It was a classmate with whom I got along well. We were both Japan-born Koreans. Her name was Yaoka Nami. Because both of us were using Japanese names as other Japan-born Koreans do, there was no way for us to know about it. For the first time in my life I could throw my mask away. I saw her doing the same. It was a refreshing experience.

We Japan-born Koreans easily blend into Japanese society because of physical similarity. Fortunately, or unfortunately, we just cannot know, even when we see the person every day. I was impressed several years ago when I saw African-Americans greeting each other 'Hi brother,' 'Sister,' confirming their solidarity.

When she was in Korea:

It was particularly joyful to meet and know Japan-born Koreans. We were all using our real names without feeling intimidated. Yes, for the first time in my life I held a Korean passport carrying my real name, Yumi Lee. It was so easy to use my real name in Korea (well, naturally); it was hard to imagine that I used to feel that it was 'life-threatening' to use it while going through exams in Japan.

After coming back to Japan, I revealed that I was a Japan-born Korean to my friends, including Kuro, my best friend from junior high, and Maru and Nishi, friends from college. First, I took Kuro to Maruyama Park in Kyoto to talk about it privately. Revealing my identity to my best friend felt as if I was sharing my most important secret. I could do it only because I had gained self-confidence and discovery from the study tour to Korea. Otherwise, I would never have revealed it because being a Korean in Japan is a one hundred percent negative experience. 'You are a criminal if you are a Korean' is the social atmosphere in Japan.

Kuro's reaction was rather matter-of-fact. She did not seem to be particularly surprised. She listened to me quietly. Maru and Nishi did not seem to know how to react. Nishi asked: 'So, you're not a Japanese?' It was as confusing for them as to me to understand what it meant to be a Japan-born Korean. This confusion is understandable: we study in the classroom, we see each other every day, but we are never taught what Japan-born Koreans are. Then one day one of us comes forward to tell the rest who she is and the response is: 'You just do not get it.'

Regarding the physical indistinguishability of most Japan-born Koreans (though some Korean-born types are distinctive), Yumi Lee has a few more observations:

Someone I knew told me that she was told: 'What? You are a Korean? Don't worry, you look like a Japanese.' It sounds as if being a Korean is bad. Friends assure you that it's okay, with intended consideration and sympathy for you, as if being thought Japanese is an honor.

'You are Korean? You must be kidding! There's no way anyone would ever suspect you are not a Japanese.' Japanese say this without much thought. Is it supposed to be honorable to be mistaken for a Japanese?

Yumi Lee's public 'coming out' or 'real name declaration'—a momentous rite of passage for Koreans who have resolved to maintain their ethnic identity—occurred during her tertiary course at St. Agnes Junior College.

I had an American teacher, Linda Crawford, who was the only teacher I got close to while I was at the college. Since she was a 'foreigner' she did not have any reservations. It did not matter to her whether I was a Japanese or a Korean. I talked about my trip to America and my coming out; I revealed my real name and my being a Japan-born Korean.

I was not ready that day, the day I will never forget. It was in Linda's class. Linda was calling the roll. 'Ms Tanaka.' 'Yes.' 'Ms Nakamura.' 'Yes.' It went on as usual. She then stopped just before calling my name, which had usually been called as 'Ms Uno.' There was a moment of silence. Then she said: 'Ms Uno, what should I call you from now on?' I sat frozen. I was speechless. Everything seemed to have gone blank. I did not know what to do. Nevertheless, I was not all that ready to reveal it to the whole class. It was so sudden. A strange silence prevailed. 'I am at a loss' was all I could say to her with an effort. The class must have wondered what was going on. Yet as Linda quickly went on to call the next student, the suspicious atmosphere subsided.

I myself was feeling shaky. 'Is this the moment that I stand up and say my real Korean name?' 'No, it is too hard.' 'Yes, I can do it.' My mind was occupied with battles of thought. When Linda finished calling the roll, I found myself raising my arm high. She said, 'Yes?' I replied, 'My real name is Yumi Lee. You can call me Lee from today on.'

I DID it. I could not believe it! It took my whole courage and spiritual strength. It was an incredible moment for me. Remembering that moment makes me shiver even ten years later. After the class, classmates swarmed around me and asked me about myself. I told them I was a Ko-

69

rean and that my real name was Lee. One said: 'So, you are not Japanese?' Another said: 'Your passport is not red?' Yet another said, 'So, you are from Korea?'

The truth is I was born and raised in Japan, just like the rest of my classmates. But coming out made me conspicuous. The most unforgettable day had taken place. I was boiling inside out with an inexplicable sensation. Linda had not thought it was such a big deal to ask me whether I wanted to use my real Korean name. Later on, she realized how much it meant to me.

Even now when we get together we talk about it. She has remarked: 'You must have hated me for what I did to you.' Yes, at the time I was immensely upset with the situation I was put in. But now I can laugh at it. Truly, I don't hate her at all but instead appreciate her for presenting me with such a rare chance.

What we call 'real name declaration' is, however, a serious matter. For many Koreans in Japan, it is a knee-shaking experience. As a matter of fact, more than 90 percent use their Japanese names. Occasionally, as in my case, with deep trust for one's school teacher and classmates, some young Koreans come out, often with tears—but not as unexpectedly as in my case.

How many people in the world would even think that the use of their real names is an event taking the utmost courage even inducing tears?

I went back home that day with a victorious feeling: 'I did it!' I told my father how for the first time I had used my Korean name. I felt like showing off my courage to him. I asked him: 'Why don't you use your Korean name?' What I really wanted to say was: 'I did it, why can't you? Not enough courage?' He replied: 'We've got to eat.' It was not a matter of courage, but of survival for him. My parents have to use their Japanese names to keep their business. It's not a matter of choice. This reality confronted me. After I had used up my courage to use my Korean name, I was confronted with this reality. Some people have no choice about their names. I know deep inside that my parents were proud of me using my Korean name, although they must have anticipated the consequences.

The use of Korean names is so unusual among long-term residents that anyone using theirs is assumed to be a recent arrival or a transient. This is illustrated by the occasion when Yumi Lee was taken to hospital after a domestic accident.

I was taken to the hospital, where I gave my name to a nurse. She assumed that I was not a Japanese and started to speak to me slowly on purpose. After the medical examination, she handed me a piece of paper

70

with advice. She started to read the paper to me as if talking to a baby. I said, 'I understand Japanese.' She kept on being nice. 'You ... need ... to ... stay ... completely ... rested ... for ... a ... while.... If ... you ... feel ... ill ... you ... have ... to ... come again ...

She kept on reading slowly like this, as if to comfort me. I was like a poor foreigner. 'Enough: Quit it! I know Japanese!' I thought. I managed to keep quiet. She was innocently nice. To me, it was another humiliation. If I used my alias, it would have been different. She would have treated me like an *ordinary* Japanese.

Recently I have started to use both my names, depending on the situation, to be free of these kinds of mental torment. My Korean friends agree. 'You cannot always put yourself in such a position to be vulnerable to frustration.'

What would an American do if he was addressed in pidgin English just because he has, say, an Italian name? This shows how naive Japanese society is. If someone has a name of foreign origin, he is not a Japanese and is therefore handicapped in terms of the language.

The general Japanese public love to figure out who are ethnic Koreans among known TV celebrities. Clues are particular names that Koreans tend to use and particular places of birth. Once they figure that out, the news would be released sensationally. He would be pointed out, 'he is a Korean!' It is equivalent to singling out a Jew in America, 'A is a Jew!' Almost no Korean celebrities, thus, come out in Japan for fear of discrimination.

Each resident Korean reserves his or her feelings towards names. I had the chance to come out. Some would never have the choice. If we had a free choice without facing discrimination, we would use our real names without hesitation. Society is severe on us. Even if we once come out, provided with support and understanding at school, we are sometimes forced back to our Japanese names by invisible, or sometimes visible, pressure when we are looking for a job. A name is not a simple matter for us. One does not declare one's real name easily. We cannot lightly surrender that hard-won identity for Japanese names, even when forced to do so. Reusing the Japanese name has a more psychologically negative impact than the declaration itself.

My cousin, who graduated from a famous university in Kansai, went out job hunting with his real name. A ranking enterprise was interested in him as a prospective candidate. In the final interview, the interviewer told him, 'we would like you to use your Japanese name in our company, not your Korean name, Park.' This is common. But he felt this was a blatant insult to him, and gave up the opportunity to join that company. I am sure that there are a number who take a Japanese name to get a job by killing their own identity. However, he seems full of life.

Cheers to him! In Japan, Koreans are particularly excluded from sales departments. The company considers how the clients would react. They do not want Koreans to use their real names because they may lose sales for the store.

Cases where Korean businessmen confidently use their real names are felt as an occasion for celebration.

> Ako, my youngest sister, ran into a friend of hers, a Korean, on the street. He works for a real estate agency nearby. She came home very excited. 'Look, Yumi, look at his business card. Gon uses his real name.' His business card reads 'Gon,' with Japanese phonetic letters (*kana*) to indicate the Korean pronunciation of the Chinese character used for his name. To me, it seemed to shine. We clapped our hands. 'This is great!' Then, it hit me. We are in a society where we are enormously impressed when we see someone using his real name at the office. Using one's real name should be natural. [This incident took place on 29 October 1994.]

Some cases of a more ceremonial form of real name declaration are described in *Why do Koreans take Japanese Names?* by Kim Il-myon (1978). Kim is a prolific and eloquent writer on the problems of the Korean community in Japan. He is the author of the most comprehensive collection of wartime reminiscences by Japanese servicemen on 'comfort women,' entitled *The Emperor's Forces and Korean Comfort Women*. His study of the names issue is also the most exhaustive available. The rituals he describes occurred in primary schools in the Osaka area from 1974, where they were stimulated first by the general raising of Korean consciousness following the Hitachi Case and secondly by the Liberationist Education Movement. This was a group which fought for the betterment of Korean and Burakumin individuals and was especially influential among teachers.

The first recorded case occurred in December 1974 and took the form of an oath by a final year pupil declaimed in the assembly hall before the teaching staff and all 620 pupils. About one-fifth, or121, of the pupils were Korean (a standard percentage for this area). The oath went:

> I am a Korean called Lee. From now on I mean to have confidence in being Korean and to enlist everyone to fight discrimination, to fight to recover our language, and to recover pride in our history. I declare this before all of you. I wish all of you, both Japanese and Koreans, to freely call me Lee whether we are playing or at any other time.

72

This was, as Kim suggests, a comprehensive declaration of struggle against discrimination and for ethnic awakening among Koreans. The ground had been prepared by the distribution to all parents, in the principal's name, of a circular entitled 'Education to Eliminate Discrimination.'

In this case, however, the pupil's own mother was not convinced of the wisdom of the move. She had tried up until the day before to dissuade him from going ahead. She was 35 and had been born in Japan. She accused her son of 'just trying to be a big hero' and of exposing her Korean identity: now she would be known as 'the boy Lee's mother.' In many other cases, however, the parents came to follow their children's example and openly declare a Korean identity. Meanwhile, the children's performance at school was said to be improved through a new-found confidence.

There were, of course, negative effects. Some Japanese nationalists told their children not to play with declared Koreans, while others, both Japanese and Koreans, transferred their children to less progressive schools to avoid confrontation. The Osaka city school board circulated a notice at this time that Korean children's real names were to be used in official records, with the Korean pronunciation indicated in *kana*. The degree of compliance may have been limited. Later accounts indicate the practice as being more widely taken up with the fuller recognition of ethnic education in 1991, following the Memoire with South Korea.

Such oaths were often difficult to maintain on entry to secondary education, where Korean numbers were smaller and support groups less effective. The situation became more difficult when the student entered the job market.

Kim describes the dilemma the Koreans faced after noting that the adoption of local names by immigrants in other countries is common enough:

> However, the use of Japanese aliases by Koreans living in Japan far exceeds this in significance. It may be viewed at first sight as a mere matter of naming but is so deep-rooted that, when its background is explored, the real-life situation of Koreans who have come to be in Japan, and the environment of Japanese society itself, are brought into sharp relief. When it is abstracted and comprehended as a general issue, it raises the question of Japanese social discrimination and bias against Koreans, as well as confronting the ethnic consciousness of the Koreans themselves as one bereft of real identity.
>
> The Japanese aliases for some of the Koreans form an expedient for camouflaging themselves or an element of protective coloring like that of the tree frog. It is an expedient for avoiding the thorns of frontal attack by a discriminatory society.
>
> There are not a few examples of people becoming aware of their Korean nationality for the first time when confronted with barriers to employment or marriage. They may then tackle their parents with: 'Why

did you bring us up in the guise of Japanese?' Some boys, encountering the barrier of cruel discrimination, despair and become delinquent and finish up joining criminal gangs.

Those who retain their aliases and successfully enter the workforce have to conceal their family circumstances, even to the extent of concealing the very existence of their Korean parents.

As examples of this situation, Kim gives the case of an aged mother coming to visit her son who is passing as Japanese. To avoid betraying her Korean character, the family tried not to let the mother out of the house. She, of course, was interested in seeing something of unfamiliar Japan and wanted to stroll about. The family took the precaution of dressing her in a skirt and sweater instead of her customary Korean costume. Before long, she began to feel out of place. Eventually she returned to Korea, at which her son expressed a mixture of distress and relief.

Kim also cited a case involving an aged Korean father who lived with his married and largely assimilated daughter. She developed Japanese social tastes, such as joining tea ceremony or flower arrangement clubs, necessarily involving bringing frequent visitors to the house. She then had to keep her father out of the way because if he was heard to speak, his Korean accent would be obvious or else his breath would smell of garlic. What must be the cost of such subterfuge?

One famous case was that of a TV star who, when interviewed about her background at the time she was beginning to become famous, said that her father had been killed in the War—even though he was still alive. Her father consented to this deceit rather than spoil her career by revealing her Korean ancestry. As a Japanese writer commented later when the truth came out: 'It is we Japanese who have set the stage for such a lie to be told.'

One remarkable case of identity concealment for business purposes goes back to 1957 when Kim himself, after a gap of 20 or more years, learned the address of a relative whom he had known in their teenage years in their home town in Korea. He visited his relative in Kobe, where he found he had done well in the construction business. In Japan, this business exists on the fringes of the underworld and is influenced by its codes. Kim's relative was a labor gang boss controlling scores of laborers. Kim describes him as massively built, his suntanned hands hard as rock and his arms thick as poles from his hard life. He had four children by a Japanese wife. He had forgotten most of his Korean and had long lived without contact with Korean people or organizations. The name plate on his fine new house read Ishida Taro, a quite commonplace Japanese name.

When his children came home from primary school, they were excited to see a relative of their father's, as up to then they had only met their mother's family. The little daughter asked what was her 'uncle's' name and, on being told it was Kim, was puzzled, partly at its strangeness and partly because it should have been Ishida. Kim's host then told the child that her mother wanted her and, when she was gone, proceeded to tell Kim his story, first closing the window and turning on a radio so that they could not be overheard.

He explained that he had long passed as Ishida Taro, a Japanese, and that his children had no idea of his Korean origin. He had not at first set out to conceal this, but as his life led him among Japanese and away from Koreans, this identity had gradually taken over. When Kim showed surprise at noticing a photograph of the Crown Prince over the door lintel—something unusual even in Japanese homes at that time when patriotism was at an ebb—his host explained that his elder daughter had to buy it at school, and her friends would expect to see it when they visited her. He went on to emphasize that he had not changed at heart. He produced his Alien Registration card to demonstrate that he had not naturalized and 'sold' out.

By way of indicating how essential a Japanese identity was for the sake of the family's livelihood, he outlined the nature of his business. His situation was typical in his field, where the pervasive paternalism of Japanese society retains its most feudal form. He subcontracted for a large construction company and received commissions of 8 percent to 10 percent, consisting of deductions from the daily wages of his laborers, which at that time came to about ¥1,000 per day. From this, however, he had to cover his workers for accidents; one had cost him ¥80,000. He had to display the drive and toughness needed both to spur on and to control his team.

Kim reflected that his friend certainly had the necessary qualities, both psychological and physical. At home in Korea, he had been the strongest boy in the village, able to carry a five-bushel sack of rice easily at the age of sixteen. He had come to Japan at eighteen, worked in construction, married, and had his first daughter at the end of the Second World War. In the subsequent chaos, his restless energies found an outlet in the black market. He was not a mere peddler but an organizer, shipping mainly rice and tobacco from Shikoku to the shattered remnants of Osaka, employing buyers on the island, distributors in the city, and boatmen to cross the straits. He had become known by this time as 'boss Ishida.' He planned to build a cinema and run it for a more stable livelihood but was defrauded of the funds.

As post-war stability returned, he moved back into construction. To become a labor gang boss, he had to be physically powerful, have a fighting spirit and stern resolution, and be able to lead the way in risky operations. At the same time, he needed to be generous when appropriate. He apparently had what it took. Some of his younger subordinates were intensely devoted to him, speaking of being ready to die for him if need be. They wore tattoos like *yakuza* and were feared in their quarter of Kobe. In his presence, however, they were like 'mice in front of a cat.' They did not know he was a Korean.

75

Some of his subordinates were ex-convicts, prone to murderous fights with construction tools. His authority was usually sufficient to stop them. Yet all his hard-won authority might crumble if he were known to be Korean. If he sometimes longed for the traditional dish of white cabbage pickled with garlic, the smell of his breath might start his workers wondering about his identity. As he put it:

> The one they follow so docilely is their Boss Ishida, not someone who has come across from Korea. That is all there is to it. You may think that I have a good, settled life as a construction boss but inwardly I am never at ease.
>
> Up to the age of thirty, I was tough enough to be afraid of nothing, but now that I am past forty, fighting seems pointless. My health has suffered too. I used to drink a three pint bottle of sake every day after I came home from work, but I've ruined my stomach and can't live without stomach medicine. If you get old and your health declines, you can't carry much weight any more.
>
> You're finished if you betray any sign of weakness. I can't take medicine in front of them. With their peculiar psychology, they think that if the boss can't drink sake any more it's a sign that he is in decline, so I have even had to drink water from a sake bottle when they have been looking.

Not long after his visit, Kim heard that his relative had naturalized—presumably in the hope that this would provide him with some insurance against the weakness of age.

Legal initiatives to reclaim names

Some naturalized Koreans have begun a campaign to revert legally to their Korean names. This began in the summer of 1982 at the Third National Research Conference on Korean Education in Japan. Some of the participants, although naturalized under varied circumstances and, bearing Japanese names as then required, had not rejected their ethnicity and used their Korean names informally. This was a mirror image of non-naturalized Koreans using Japanese aliases and sometimes being more assimilated in practice than the ethnically conscious naturalized. The latter group at the conference raised the possibility of having their Korean names legally recognized.

These people met again later in the year at the annual conference of the Mintoren. Professor Tanaka Hiroshi, an energetic and vocal activist for better relations with Asians, became their regular advisor. During his post-graduate days, he had served in the Asian Students' Cultural Association and was head of a university faculty of foreign languages. The group held monthly study

76

meetings at the home of an Osaka member to explore the labyrinthine legal and social implications of their proposal. Although, as noted, the strictly legal grounds for naturalization did not specify the adoption of Japanese names, administrative discretion was final, and this requirement was laid down in the Guide to Naturalization Procedures. Some hesitated to pursue the matter in case it might promote naturalization. To avoid this, they categorized themselves as 'Koreans of Japanese Nationality.'

They were encouraged by two test cases. One was that of a Vietnamese named Tran Dinh-tong who had been naturalized under a Japanese name but was permitted by the Kobe Family Court to resume his original name on 'grounds of unavoidable necessity.' As usual, lower level or local authorities have been the main source of liberalizing tendencies. The group also uncovered another case, not reported in the media, where the Sakai branch of the Osaka Family Court had done the same for one Pang Chong-nam of mixed Japan-Korean parentage. These decisions did not represent clear-cut precedents but gave hints of possible approaches.

In 1983, the first initiative was taken in the Kawasaki branch of the Yokohama Family Court by Yun Cho-ja. (*Minzokumei o Torimodosu Kai* 1990). Her case was distinctive in that, being the daughter of a Korean father and a Japanese mother, she had acquired Japanese nationality at birth by being registered as illegitimate on her mother's Domicile Register—a not uncommon practice where this is thought to be in the child's interests. (Although movement within Japan is free and does not require registering, every Japanese national has to have a basic Domicile Registration in their place of origin with the local municipal office.)

Her father is described as agreeing with her concealment of his paternity. He had been brought to Japan as a child. His own father had made a living as a night-soil collector, charcoal seller, and raw sake dealer, but Cho-ja's father was talented enough to become a professional musician. His wife had married him for love and was then disowned by her family. They separated when Cho-ja was aged seven. She was then brought up by her mother's family as a Japanese (her name Cho-ja being pronounced Japanese style as Teruko). She had only a vague idea of her background. At school she passed as Japanese, though she remembers derogatory remarks comparing her to Koreans being directed at her although the others did not know that her father was Korean. She remembers, for example, that when she wore her hair parted in the center, students would scoff at a 'Korean-parting;' if she wore bright green they would describe it as 'Korean colored.'

She had some contact with Koreans when attending a folk-dance and cultural festival at an ethnic secondary school and at a Japanese-Korean student's club. After this she came to feel more affinity with Koreans. In her English studies, she came across the word 'cosmopolitan' and felt that it described her outlook. After this, she began to reveal her Korean identity. She found no adverse reactions, and one friend told her that she need not have been so furtive.

On graduation, she was employed at a school for handicapped children. After the Hitachi case she became a volunteer with the Korean welfare organization, the Seikyusha (in Korean Chonggusa, or Green Hills Society, after a traditional epithet of Korea. Green Hills was the Chinese name for a mythical land of immortals in the East.). This gave her deeper associations with the Korean community, and when she transferred to a primary school with a large number of Korean children, she began to use her Korean name professionally. This caused some tensions, but the principal finally decided in her favor.

Cho-ja is eloquent about her aims, which primarily mean challenging the 'myth of the unitary (or totally homogeneous) nation,' in which even part-Japanese tend to be rejected as 'not proper Japanese' no matter how well adjusted they are to Japanese society. She notes, however, that the Korean community also tends to be exclusive, so that part-Koreans, no matter how sympathetic they are to Korean causes, are admitted only to lower-level organizations. Some Koreans dismiss names as an issue, asserting that what matters is content not names. But, she asks, what defines content? To her, the names struggle is the struggle against discrimination. She had been criticized by Korean nationals and Leftists on the grounds that, having Japanese nationality, she is actually spared the trials associated with alien registration.

To this she replies:

> I feel impatient when resident Koreans themselves make a fetish of nationality, which has either been thrust upon them or stripped away as an instrument of control and division. I think they are under an illusion when they regard ethnic identity as being simply a matter of retaining a nationality. They imagine they can preserve their attenuating ethnicity just by hanging on to a nationality tag. By casting off those with Japanese nationality, we have caused endless dissension within our community and impeded ethnic solidarity.
>
> I do not urge anyone to renounce a nationality. I think it is proper to ask what is wrong with retaining the nationality one was born with. This applies to my case too, as I have had Japanese nationality since birth. Nationality and ethnicity are distinct. The important thing is to view nationality as relative.

When she launched her case, the court examiner tried to dissuade her from persisting by arguing that when she married her surname would be changed in any case, so what was the point? She argued that she wished to bear the name that would have normally been hers in the absence of social discrimination—that is, her father's name. But she lost her case.

When she did marry, she married a Japanese teacher who taught mainly Korean children. She did not register the marriage in the Domicile Registration, so that their surnames could be kept separate and children would be registered under hers. 'The Domicile Registration System is what maintains discrimination, whether against Burakumin, Koreans, or illegitimate children,' she says. They had two children who were given names from the limited number available that, like Yumi Lee's, would be pronounced alike in both languages. They began their education at the Seikyusha Nursery School under the mother's Korean name, Yun. The mother's hope was that her children would take pride in 'spanning two cultures, in being of mixed ancestry, with Japanese nationality and Korean names.'

Pak Sil made the next attempt at the Kyoto Family Court in 1984. His parents had come to Japan in the 1920s and, as was common among the Pak clan, passed under the Japanese name Arai. His eldest brother succeeded in subcontracting, married a Japanese, and naturalized after the Peace Treaty. His elder sister passed an employment examination for a large electric company but, as in the later Hitachi Case, was rejected when her nationality was disclosed. She then made two suicide attempts, which left her permanently incapacitated. Sil himself followed the common pattern of successfully passing in a small electricity business where he had to listen to the standard abuse exchanged among Japanese about Koreans such as: 'Are you a fool or a Korean?' or 'I don't deal with fools or Koreans.'

Sil became more conscious of Korean issues through the campaigns of the late 1960s on the Immigration Control Bills. He began to study their historical background, but this course was deflected for a time by a love marriage to a Japanese girl. They met at church and agreed to marry. [see Religion, Chap. 15 below] Sil then visited her parents in Yamaguchi at the Western extremity of Honshu. This is an area noted for conservatism. The girl's parents were horrified by the idea of marriage to a Korean. When the daughter persisted, her mother attempted suicide.

There followed long months of wrangling within the family until the father proposed as a compromise that Sil be naturalized and that he himself would disown his daughter. This would mean that she would be struck off the family's Domicile Register and be transferred to Sil's when he was naturalized. This would avoid the question of formal consent to her marriage but meant that she could have no further contact with her family.

Sil at first hesitated to naturalize because of his dawning consciousness of the Korean question. He finally agreed for the sake of both love and honor. The couple returned to Kyoto where, pending the tortuous process of his naturalization, he could not obtain accommodation as a Korean but managed to do so in her name. (Yumi Lee also finds it impossible to find accommodation in Kyoto under her own name.) Finally, he cleared all the naturalization hurdles, and had his family alias Arai legalized and his given name Sil rendered in its Japanese form, Minoru.

The couple had three children, and during the process of their growth and schooling, he came to regret the loss of his Korean heritage. He studied Korean as well as other aspects of his culture and, although mistrusted by some Koreans as a turncoat, he managed to become a teacher in an ethnic school.

With the full support of his Japanese wife, he decided to apply to have the children's names in Korean form accepted for general use at school. The children agreed, though they suffered some teasing. One remarked once that her mother was lucky to have only a Japanese name. At this the mother, to show solidarity with her daughter, began habitual use of the surname Pak as well, which Sil was also doing.

In his court proceedings, Sil based his case on the clause in the Domicile Registration Law referring to 'grounds of unavoidable necessity'—but the court threw out his case. The judgment held that such grounds were not constituted either by the inconvenience arising from the use of two sets of names, which had arisen from personal choice, or by the wish to preserve an ethnic heritage.

The next attempt was made by Chong Yang-i at the Osaka Family Court in 1985. Both his parents had been born in Japan and spoke only broken Korean. They had, however, married according to Korean custom and always ate Korean food, including *kimchi,* daily. They also maintained Korean family rites and festivals. Since they lived in a quarter with few Koreans, the two sons were enrolled in a Japanese school where Yang-i was bullied and told to 'go back to Korea.' His parents told him to insist that he was really Japanese.

Although this mollified the bullies, it depressed Yang-i. He would complain to his parents: 'Why am I the only Korean while all the others are Japanese?' Whenever Korea was mentioned in a history or geography lesson, he would check whether the others were whispering about him. Although he was extremely fond of *kimchi*, he stopped eating it after being accused of smelling of garlic.

At about the time he entered junior high school, his parents started discussing the possibility of naturalization, since aliens were denied social security and bank finance. They didn't at first pursue the matter because his grandfather was still alive—a situation often mentioned in relation to the question of naturalization. His parents considered it more seriously, however, when Yang-i's elder brother was to take the secondary school entrance examination. Although his performance qualified him for a top-ranking school, his teacher advised him to sit for a school one rank lower because of possible ethnic discrimination. This meant giving up the medical career which had been his dream. The parents then decided to naturalize to avoid further disadvantages of this kind.

In senior high school, Yang-i participated in student movements and took up Korean studies with a vengeance, since he had come to feel that the Korean community's problems were paramount. As a result, he shed his complex about being Korean and entered a university where he could major in Korean Studies. His fellow students began to pronounce his Japanese name Kato in its Korean form Hadong, which made him want to return to his original Korean name Chong. He notes the paradox that when Chong was his legal name, he had disliked using it, but he embraced it when it was no longer his legal name. He then came to envy Koreans who had not naturalized, not yet having come to the view that nationality and ethnicity need not be identical. He now condemned his parents for naturalizing him.

He sought legal advice on resuming Korean nationality but was advised that was impossible while he was a resident in Japan. He was advised that he could legally resume his Korean name 'on grounds of unavoidable necessity,' if he could prove that he had habitually used his 'Korean alias' for many years. So he saved evidence of the use of his Korean name on postal articles and other documents.

By 1985, his lawyer believed he had a strong enough case on both the grounds that he had long used his Korean alias and also in view of the amendment that year to the Nationality Law under the convention against sex discrimination. (The 1985 amendment led the way to greater flexibility in this area.) But he failed both in the initial hearing and on appeal, so he decided to broaden and publicize the issue, having discovered during the proceedings that ethnic Koreans in his situation were far more numerous than he had realized. Apart from 150,000 known to have naturalized, there were a large number of others inheriting Japanese nationality who still retained some ethnic consciousness.

His group therefore formed the Association to Recover Ethnic Names and began to issue a quarterly bulletin called *Uri Irum* (Korean for 'our names,' though the contents are in Japanese). The founding address was delivered by Professor Tanaka and local study groups were formed, together with support groups for further court action. The Association's activities also included publicity for the movement to refuse fingerprinting among Koreans with alien status.

This campaign went into high gear in 1985, when large numbers of registration renewals fell due. This helped create an atmosphere of combined action spanning both the naturalized and alien sections of the community. The *Asahi* newspaper, Japan's widely read major stronghold of liberal journalism since its foundation in the nineteenth century, reported sympathetically on the Associations' activities.

This activity contributed to the Justice Department's decision to delete the requirement for Japanese names from the Guide to Naturalization Procedure and, although in practice a strong recommendation for Japanese names persists, this did give a stronger legal argument for those who had been naturalized to reclaim their ethnic names.

In 1987, Pak Sil resubmitted his case. This time he was successful on the grounds that the requirement for a Japanese name had been deleted from the Guide and that if this situation had originally applied, he would not willingly have altered his name. Furthermore, he could now show that the family had been using the surname Pak for a number of years.

Chong Yang-i was also successful in 1987 while Yun Cho-ja resubmitted her case in 1988 and was ultimately successful, though with more delay in view of her different circumstances. An ethnic Chinese family called Liu also recovered their Chinese surname in the Osaka Family Court at the same time.

The next Korean to apply, Kim P'yong-ung, won his case in the Kyoto Family Court within two months. He had naturalized in order to qualify for a teaching position in physical training. Having graduated from the Kyoto University of Education, he was fully qualified, but because he was unwilling at first to naturalize, he was unable to obtain a teaching position and instead worked in the *pachinko* business. Eventually, he accepted naturalization as the only practical solution but later wanted to return to his Korean name when he heard of Pak Sil's case. He was advised to extend the use of his Korean name by agreement with his principal and the circulation of a memorandum of intent to do so. This facilitated his case and brought early success. Cases of this sort are slowly becoming more frequent and easier to get through the courts, but the automatic right to a choice of names remains a distant prospect.

Even when Korean names are accepted, their pronunciation still presents problems in Japan and is a source of emotional tension. Although, as mentioned earlier, proper names are written in Chinese characters in both languages, their pronunciations differ because Chinese writing is not phonetic but ideographic. Even within China itself, the pronunciation of characters varies widely. The surname read 'Wu' in Mandarin is 'Goh' in Fukienese and 'Ng' in Cantonese. In Vietnamese it becomes 'Ngo,' in Japanese 'Go' (as usual following the older southern pronunciation), and in Korean 'O,' a case of the Korean tendency to drop initials. These last two readings are described as Sino-Japanese and Sino-Korean. Japanese also has an indigenous reading which in the case of this character is 'Kure.'

Traditionally, it has been customary for each of these linguistic groups to pronounce characters in its own way. They could hardly do otherwise without having learned the other language(s). It is comparable to the way in which English speakers can only pronounce foreign names according to English phonetics unless they happen to know the language in question.

Until some time after World War II, it was regarded as normal to read Korean names, when using Japanese, in the Sino-Japanese form. Japanese names, when using Korean, would be pronounced in the Sino-Korean form. But Koreans in Japan came to feel that the Sino-Japanese readings had colonial associations and to demand that the Japanese pronounce their Korean names, when used, in the Sino-Korean way. They could not do this properly, of course, without learning Korean, but the sounds can be rendered approximately in the Japanese phonetic *kana* script, which the Koreans found acceptable. At the same time, they did not wish to discard Chinese characters because of their symbolism and other associations. They wished their names to be written with both sets of writing together.

To illustrate, the name Chong Yang-i (Sino-Korean) is read Tei Ryoji in Sino-Japanese, but in this case the *kana* script can render the Korean sounds quite well. By contrast, Pak Sil is Boku Jitsu in Sino-Japanese but in *kana* can only be approximated as Paku Shiru, since *kana* cannot write final consonants except n, and l must be replaced by r. The Koreans are satisfied with the best approximation, but many Japanese prefer the traditional system which is natural to them. In any case, they have no means of knowing the Sino-Korean pronunciation unless *kana* accompanies the Chinese characters.

The first formal dispute over this type of question occurred in 1949 when a secretary of the South Korean mission resigned from his post to live in Japan. He therefore had to register as an alien, but in his application form, instead of writing the Chinese characters for Kim Hae-song, he wrote the *kana* approximation Kimu Hae-seongu. He did this not out of anticolonialism but because he belonged to an extreme nativist movement which wished to eliminate Chinese influence from Korean culture. This tendency is actually stronger in North Korea than in the south and is about on par with an attempt to eliminate all continental influence from British culture.

The ward office pointed out that Chinese and Koreans were required to record their names in Chinese characters, as were Japanese. (This provided a clear standard that avoided the multiplicity of phonetic variants in all three languages.) But if this were done, Kim's name would be read by the Japanese as Kin Kaisei which he felt was an affront to the integrity of his name. His passion and patriotism on this issue, as with many Korean activists, was buttressed by an uncompromising form of Christianity, and he went on to lecture the head of the administrative section on the philosophical and sociological implications of the Japanese practice.

Kim pointed out that, whereas the Japanese habitually pronounced names in other countries according to local usage, such as Rondon, Pari, Roma, Mosukuwa, their Sino-Japanese pronunciation of Korean and Chinese names showed a failure to respect the dignity due to independent nations. On the individual level, he had only one name and would take legal action to defend it from distortion. His name was not going to be Japanized.

When the official pleaded that there was no precedent for a *kana* entry, Kim retorted that history consisted of a succession of unprecedented events. The Emperor was no longer the supreme power in the state, and the honorific term for his palace had been replaced by a term simply meaning his residence.

He asked whether it would be permissible to refer to the ward Mayor Nagashima (indigenous reading) as Changdo (Sino-Korean). Overpowered by this logic (or for the sake of peace), the official agreed to enter Kim's name in both *kana* and romanization, as Kim Hae Seong. He told him, however, that this was a special case and asked him to keep it confidential. He apparently did so—though the writer Kim Il-myon later learned of it.

A larger case in this area was marathon litigation involving the national broadcasting service NHK. A Korean pastor in North Kyushu, Ch'oe Ch'anghwa, launched this in 1975. He had been active in Koreans' rights activities among the large community there, originating from the local mining industry. His activities were occasionally mentioned in NHK news, where his name was rendered in the Sino-Japanese form, as Sai Shoka.

He lodged a protest with the local office of NHK, which referred it to the head office and relayed its reply. This was to the effect that NHK had attempted to use the local (i.e. Korean) pronunciation from 1948 to 1953 but found pronunciation difficult and had reverted to traditional usage. The matter would be reviewed, but any change would need to be made on a nationwide basis. Current practice would be maintained at the present stage. Ch'oe decided that he 'could not permit such an infringement of basic human rights as the alteration for the convenience of others of one's name as a symbol of one's personality.' On this basis, he sued NHK for damages 'due to the infringement of human rights.' The amount named was the token amount of ¥1, but this was to be accompanied by an apology to be published in all the major newspapers, with an undertaking to pronounce Korean names correctly in the future. Japanese colonialism was attacked at some length, recalling how the plaintiff under the imposition of Japanese names had been renamed Takayama Shoka but now rejected both this name and the Japanized form of his Korean name as Sai Shoka. The amount of ¥1, being the basic unit of currency, symbolized a person's name as the most basic of one's rights. (Kim Il-Myon 1978)

Ch'oe had already fought many local battles over the correct use of his name, which was complicated both by the difficulty of pronouncing it and the obscure character used to write it. At school, he insisted on having his three children addressed correctly, although the teachers tried to use the easier Sino-Japanese form, Sai, or alternatively adopt a Japanese alias. His youngest daughter, Martha, then in fourth year primary, was mocked by other children with puns on her name, and she pleaded with her parents to 'do something about her name.' But her father impressed on her that he was bringing up his children to confront and overcome prejudice in Japanese society. He was also well known for this attitude in the local Parents and Teachers Association, where he played a prominent role. His calling card bore romanization and *kana* as well as the Chinese characters.

He hoped to use his case for the wider purpose of gaining acceptance for Koreans as Koreans and members of society with full rights. The first must be due recognition of their correct names. He received wide publicity, through the *Asahi* and the national South Korean press. He also received a large volume of mail, equally divided between support and condemnation. Hostile letters, as usual, tended to tell him to go back to Korea if he disliked Japanese ways. Japanese writers in the *Asahi* tended to support Ch'oe's argument that all should be addressed equally in whatever way they prefer and that to ignore the wishes of Koreans suggested that power relations and South Korea's economic dependence on Japanese aid was a psychological factor.

In court, NHK argued that it was obliged to follow common Japanese usage, that Korean standard pronunciation differed between North and South (which is true), and that the phonetics of Korean were difficult for listeners to grasp or recognize. This was said to have been demonstrated by its earlier trial using Korean forms. On these points Kim Il-myon comments that bad usages should be reformed, that phonetic differences between North and South are limited and that the reason for NHK's termination of its earlier trial, in 1953, was the revival of reactionary tendencies after the Peace Treaty.

The court found in favor of NHK on the grounds that it had not misrepresented Ch'oe's name, which would have constituted disrespect, but had followed social usage which, in the case of language, takes precedent over ideology, individual, or ethnic considerations.

Upon the delivery of this judgment in 1977, Ch'oe appealed first to the Regional Higher Court and then the Supreme Court, which ruled in his favor in 1988 in the following terms:

> Names, viewed socially, have the function of distinguishing and specifying the individual in relation to others but at the same time, viewed from the side of the individual, may be described as the basis for being respected as an individual, a symbol of the individual's personality and as constituting part of the content of human rights.

By then, Ch'oe's case, together with the legislative changes bringing new flexibility to the treatment of names and other factors such as the widespread call for internationalization, had largely changed common usage in the desired direction. The court was recognizing this. At the same time, prejudices persist and the inherent complexity of the issue will tend to perpetuate problems.

6 Nationality and naturalization

Yumi Lee expresses the basic reasons why most, but far from all, of the Korean community has always been unwilling to naturalize under the conditions demanded by Japan.

Japan committed indescribable brutality and sordid acts including massacre, plunder, and rape during World War II against Asians. What is more, they do not take responsibility for what they did; they act overbearingly. This is one of the reasons why I refuse complete assimilation. Their attitude is: 'We will always allow you to be one of us.' The process of complete assimilation consists of screening to select how one can be a good Japanese national and how good it would be to leave the original ethnicity behind. The historical background is completely ignored. I believe the Naturalization Law of Japan is a denial of humanity. Unlike other countries, Japan does not separate race and nationality. There is no such expression as 'Korean-Japanese' in the manner of 'Japanese-American.'

When we look back at history, most of the Jews killed in Hitler's genocide were of German nationality and the whole world saw Hitler as the enemy. It was not an issue of nationality but of ethnicity. Those Japanese-Americans forced to move into camps during World War II had American citizenship. Should tension between Japan and our mother country arise in the future, it is apparent that having Japanese nationality would not settle the problem whether for second, third, fourth, fifth, and sixth generations of resident Koreans. Japan has to review history thoroughly to understand why we are here in Japan. They have to understand, accept, and adopt an affirmative scheme. Otherwise we continue to fear the possibility the Jews once faced.

To survive and live in Japan, some obtained Japanese nationality; they went through an inhumane procedure. They are officially called 'new Japanese.' [This refers to the entry 'naturalized' on the new Domicile Register in lieu of the 'previous domicile' entry in a case of domicile transfer.]

I don't think those who become 'new Japanese' are much impressed by this procedure. Japan unreasonably emphasizes the 'favor' done to us by making us go through difficult procedures to obtain Japanese nationality. I cannot feel that Japan is a country with a big heart. Japanese nationality is not attractive to obtain. I do not want to be part of a nation which tormented, and is still tormenting, fellow Asians. In any case, Japanese nationality should be given unconditionally to permanent residents. This can be historically justified.

Intentionally, I did not apply for naturalization. I am not willing to clear those heavy conditions to make me feel I would be given something honorable. The majority of Korean residents do not become naturalized for this reason. This seems to be difficult for Westerners to understand. I'd rather live with walls of discrimination than live with falsehood.

I believe that the whole issue would become a non-issue for me when the sacrifice by my ancestors, grandparents, and parents to Japan is clarified, and sincere and appropriate compensation is made. When Japan matures, I think ill-feeling towards it will evaporate. It will not matter whether you are Japanese, resident Korean, or naturalized.

Because she has been an activist for Korean causes, Lee feels that she would not be granted Japanese nationality even if she applied.

The actual procedures for naturalization are much more complex than implied in the formal legislation. Much is left to the discretion of the Justice Minister. The law specifies that an alien is eligible for naturalization when he or she:

(1)   has lived in Japan for five or more years consecutively;
(2)   is twenty years of age or more and a person of full capacity under the law of his or her native country;
(3)   is of good character;
(4)   has property or ability adequate to lead an independent life;
(5)   has no nationality or would lose his or her former nationality upon taking Japanese nationality;
(6)   has never planned or taken part in insurgency against the Japanese state.

Let us look at how this procedure worked for Pak Sil, a Korean who applied in 1970:

87

After applying, I was repeatedly summoned to the Justice Ministry Bureau and had to submit detailed documents on such particulars as my personal history, family, relatives in South Korea, associates, property and real estate, books I owned, layout of my residence and access to it, details of my deposits and savings, the personal particulars of both my fiancee's parents and her elder brother even though we were not yet married. Then, a few days later, to make a thorough check on the accuracy of my statements, Justice Bureau officials and foreign affairs investigators visited my place of work, my neighborhood, and my friends' homes as well as my own.

Regarding my intended name after naturalization, it was explained to me, as in the Guide, that I could use my existing Japanese aliases or a new name, which could be entered in *kana*, but had to be a Japanese-style name. Though unenthusiastic, I entered the name Arai which my relatives had used since the imposition of Japanese names. Then I was led into another room where prints of all ten fingers were taken with sticky ink. Though feeling humiliated, I did as instructed.

His naturalization took a year to approve. He was personally congratulated by the Bureau chief, who mentioned that his brother and family had also become worthy Japanese nationals. (*Minzokumei o torimodosu Kai* 1990)

Although the requirement for a Japanese style name has now been deleted, it remained a requirement that the name intended after naturalization be submitted with the original application. This amounts to informal pressure to adopt a Japanese name.

The 1984 revision of the Nationality Law has abolished fingerprinting and introduced sex equality.

Let us look at the experience of a Korean woman who contemplated naturalization because she was to marry a Japanese. An attorney advised her intended husband that the application should read something like this: 'I was born and raised in Japan and have no intention of living in Korea. I have married a Japanese, had a child and love Japan.' What this woman actually wrote was different. It implied: 'I do not like Japan but for practical purposes of life I want to naturalize.' This departed too much from the recommended format, but she refused to compromise and instead withdrew her application.

Motives for naturalization can vary widely, but perhaps the most widely mentioned motive is concern for one's children's future. A typical view is that 'although the children are South Korean nationals, they know nothing of Korea and could never live there, so Korean nationality only imposes a handicap. They must have Japanese nationality in order to enter a good school and pursue an elite course.' Another negative factor is disillusionment with the rivalry between Soren and Mindan or other internal divisions or conflicts in the Korean community. According to statistics from the Justice Ministry, the total number of Koreans naturalized in Japan to 1992 was 168,456.

One issue bearing on nationality is the fate of ethnic Koreans incapacitated through war service with the Japanese armed forces. For the most part they have been neglected and disowned. As mentioned, under the Normalization Treaty of 1965 with South Korea, Japan provided funds which the ROK government could use to meet compensation claims by residents of that country. Money was distributed under the Civil Claims on Japan Application Law of 1971 and the Compensation Law of 1974. These covered about 8,500 cases. In 1987, Japan also paid a solatium of ¥2 million each to the bereaved families of Taiwanese war dead. Korean residents of Japan were, however, excluded from these measures. Only a small number benefited under the Special Relief Act for War Wounded and Bereaved which was passed by the Diet immediately after the ratification of the Peace Treaty, in 1952.

Under Occupation orders, war service pensions had been abolished at that time so that ex-servicemen would not be in a privileged position in relation to the general population. All cases of need were supposedly equally covered by the Livelihood Protection Law. But after the Peace Treaty, the interests of ex-servicemen were again provided for by a series of laws such as the Special Relief Act and restored pensions. The Special Relief Act excluded categories who had lost Japanese nationality or who lacked a Japanese Domicile Register—that is, Koreans and Taiwanese—but under a ruling by the Welfare Ministry, these were able to gain eligibility by naturalizing. A limited number did so, but for Koreans this option was canceled under the Normalization Treaty on the basis that this settled all claims by Koreans on Japan.

In the early 1990s, some Korean ex-servicemen filed lawsuits to claim compensation. Yumi Lee joined the support group of one case and describes its progress:

On 31 January 1991, Mr. Chung Sang-gun filed a suit against the Japanese government. He is a first generation Korean resident who resides in East Osaka. He filed a suit at Osaka District Court seeking the application of the Protection Law for the Wounded and the Families of Bereaved During the War and national compensation. He was one of the Koreans who were drafted as a military employee [paramilitary] for the Japanese Army during the Pacific War. He was dispatched to the Marshall Islands, was seriously injured and his right arm was amputated. The Japanese government introduced full compensation for Japanese former soldiers and military employees but they excluded resident Koreans.

Mr. Chung himself says: 'I appeal. The War is not finished yet. I am angry. The Japanese government during the War insisted on 'united Japanese and Koreans as subjects of the Imperial family.' But they ignored us after the war, claiming that 'Koreans are foreigners.' I want to talk in court about the feelings I have held for forty-five years.

Yumi Lee's support group held a public demonstration with loudspeakers and banners to draw public attention. They demanded, first, a formal apology and compensation from the Japanese government to resident Koreans (both North and South affiliated) who were former soldiers and military employees. Second, they demanded abolition of the nationality and Domicile Register articles from the Protection Law.

A similar lawsuit was filed at the same time in Tokyo by Sok Song-gi, who had been drafted into the Navy and in 1944—also in the Marshall Islands— had lost his right hand in aerial strafing. He had been brought back to the naval hospital at the Yokosuka base after the War and was later joined by his wife and daughter from Korea. They made a precarious living by collecting junk to be recycled. Sok Song-gi had been incapacitated and hospitalized for some years prior to taking up the lawsuit. He came straight from the hospital, in a wheelchair, to attend a press conference. The total compensation claimed came to ¥140 million, which would have been the amount paid in pensions to a Japanese ex-serviceman in the same condition over the intervening 38 years since the War.

His case was dismissed in July 1994 on the grounds of provisions in the Normalization Treaty. The judge, in his summing up, however, criticized the legislature for not remedying such an anomalous situation. Sok planned an appeal but died soon afterwards.

7 Alien Registration and immigration control

Koreans often regard the post-war attitude of officialdom in Japan to resident aliens as typified by a remark from a councilor in Immigration Control at the conclusion of the Peace Treaty in 1952: 'We can now have aliens served up boiled or grilled as we choose.' This is actually an adaptation of a proverbial saying applied to a person one despairs of getting the better of: 'I can't manage him either boiled or grilled.' Its meaning is probably best conveyed in English as 'We've got them where we want them.'

The decades that have passed since 1952 confirm the basic truth of this, although gradual improvements have occurred as a result both of international pressures and action by the Korean community.

Yumi Lee recalls her early experience of the Alien Registration system:

> A notice from the ward office in 1980, requesting me to register there, first informed me that I was an alien. I was sixteen years old. My father accompanied me. We went to the section with the sign 'Alien Registration.' As instructed, I presented a picture of myself, filled in the form and let them take my fingerprints. The officer in charge placed my index finger on the blank ink and pressed it again and again, with force. I felt uncomfortable, and powerless. I did everything as they ordered.
>
> Five years later, when I had to re-register, I resisted. Japan-born Koreans always know that they are somehow different from the rest of the population, and that the difference is not favorable. Then we receive a notice of Alien Registration which forces us to realize that we are officially alien.
>
> Later I found that Alien Registration had the authority legally to 'tie down' Koreans. I was supposed to carry the registration card at all times. At first, I didn't care much about the regulation and neglected to carry the card to school. When I started to become active in the movement against this regulation, I learned about the heavy punishment imposed on those who do not carry it. For instance, a young Korean man who

91

went out to buy canned juice at a vending machine around the corner was stopped by the police. He was not carrying his Alien Registration card and was taken into custody.

The requirement to carry an Alien Registration card complicates life in unexpected ways. On one occasion, Lee needed urgent hospitalization:

> Suddenly I remembered that I was not carrying my Alien Registration card, 'Oh, no! I forgot my Alien Registration card!' It came to my mind when I was suffering severe pain, not properly dressed, and in the ambulance. It made me so sad that my eyes were filled with tears. This incident symbolizes how Alien Registration mentally torments us. It is a symbol of shame, not ours but Japan's. I was deeply moved when I saw a scene in a movie about Gandhi. In South Africa, in the early 1900s, he set fire to his alien card. In the 1990s we Japan-born Koreans are still tied down by our Alien Registration card.

In 1987, Yumi Lee was planning to study in Britain.

> Before my departure I had to do one thing—renew my Alien Registration card. I received a notice from the ward office at the end of 1986. It required not only a photo and documents, but also my fingerprints once again. Since 1985 there had been a movement to refuse fingerprinting, something I supported in principle—some friends of mine refused to be fingerprinted and were arrested and physically abused. I participated in meetings to protest.
>
> I visited the ward office at the end of 1986, with my sister, who also had to renew her registration, and who also intended to refuse to be fingerprinted. I went to the window with the sign 'Alien Registration.' I felt guilty—an inexplicable feeling. How many Japanese know that resident Koreans have to drag themselves to this window feeling guilty? This is happening totally out of their sight. The person in charge came to the window. He started to proceed mechanically. 'I would like to talk to you,' I said. He replied: 'Please finish your procedure first.' No expression on his face. He took out an application form and was getting ready for fingerprinting. I told him of my intention to refuse to be fingerprinted. 'We resident Koreans have lived in Japan for generations. Why should we be treated like criminals? In Japan, criminals are the only ones whose fingerprints are taken,' I protested. I was not going to be kept silent. He kept saying: 'This is the system,' as if there were no other words. At the end, he said: 'This is my job.' The expression on his face said: 'Don't give me any trouble.'

Of course. He must think of his family. He is no doubt a husband and father. His duty was to proceed with the allotted task at this window. I could not give way, although I could sympathize with him. 'Let me see the chief of this section,' I said. He went into a back room. The chief invited me into a guest room. I tried to calm myself so that I could talk. The manager was nonchalantly calm. He said to my sister and me, 'I'll listen to what you have to say.' 'Why are we forced to give our fingerprints? It is illogical from a historical viewpoint for us resident Koreans to be treated in this way.' 'This is how we are instructed by the government,' he said. 'I am not going to give my fingerprints. It is absolutely unreasonable. What do you personally think about fingerprinting?' I asked. 'Personally, I understand your point. However, this is the country's system, and it is my responsibility to instruct applicants to do so. I ask you to do it this time just as you did last time.'

Despite my protests, and although I did the best I could, the chief, just like the person at the window, was mechanical. 'We are doing this because it is our job.' A typical answer, speaking on the authority of the country. I refused to be fingerprinted and my sister and I went home.

In the 1980s, resident Koreans broke their silence. The movement to refuse fingerprinting developed by itself like a small stone thrown into a pond which has a ripple effect. This movement peaked in 1985.

Mr. Han Chong-sok threw the first stone in the Shinjuku (Tokyo) ward office in September 1980. His was a 'lone rebellion.' Others followed him, first, one by one, then spreading out. If there are ten fingerprint refusers, there are ten different reasons. Mr. Han is first generation. A younger generation has its own story. One protester had seen Japanese kids bullying a Korean kid. Out of fear that he might be bullied if his ethnicity were revealed, he joined in the bullying. He confessed this bitter memory when he joined the movement.

Another, a female university student, remembers: 'I gave my fingerprints, reasoning to myself that I should put up with such a marginal matter because I am a Korean.' She continues, 'I want to live as I am, being honest to myself. When I recall it, I realized I greatly suppressed some part of myself. After refusing fingerprinting, I was told by my friends that I became more cheerful.'

Yumi Lee's determination to avoid fingerprinting was complicated by her desire to travel abroad. She planned a trip to Britain but would not be able to obtain a re-entry permit into Japan unless she submitted to fingerprinting prior to her departure date.

Although we are not immigrants, the Immigration Control Law is applied to us. Additionally, in those days the permit was good for only one year. When we wanted to stay abroad as students, for example, we had to return to Japan once a year to obtain a re-entry permit. And if you were a fingerprint refuser, your name was entered on a criminal list. One might leave Japan but risk being deprived of the permanent residence permit.

Yumi Lee was accompanied to the ward office by an American friend. Faced with the necessity to have her fingerprints taken if she wished to travel abroad and then return, she hesitated, until her American friend told her: 'They can take away your fingerprints but not your dignity.' After convincing herself of what he said, she let the official take her fingerprints.

In the 1980s when the movement to refuse fingerprinting came on the scene, the Japanese unintentionally dropped their mask. I know how much courage and resolution it took to refuse fingerprinting. I have gone through it when I tried. There were a number of Koreans who did not agree with fingerprinting but could not participate in the protest movement.

Yumi Lee's experiences and feelings are supported by those of many others. The anomaly of deportation to South Korea of a member of a later generation born in Japan was forcefully expressed by Sin Kyong-hwan in the first such case to occur after the Normalization Treaty. Sin, whose prospects for a business career were ruined by anti-Korean bias, despite his good academic record, fell into crime. He was sentenced to eight years imprisonment, which under the Treaty left him liable to deportation. But being a model prisoner, he was given a parole after five years. He took court action to contest his deportation. As he stated his case:

I committed a crime. The penalty was eight years imprisonment. I have no complaint about that but I utterly refuse to accept deportation. I am a product of Japan's aggression. Without Japan's aggression on Korea, I would never have been in Japan. It is not my responsibility that I am now resident in Japan, but that of the Japanese government. In order to conceal this, the government is trying to deport me. The status and basis (even if not very great) which our parents built up with their blood and tears as a legacy to later generations must not be allowed to come to nothing. We later generations must endeavor to put down firm roots on this basis.

Through the efforts of his support group in this litigation, the Justice Minister canceled his deportation order and cases of this kind are not expected to recur (Min 1994).

Alien Registration, which has to be maintained up to date in the municipality of current residence, partly serves the same civil functions as the Japanese

94

nationals' Residents' Basic Register. It is, however, distinguished from the latter by the requirement constantly to carry the registration card, which turns it into an instrument of close surveillance. It has to be presented 'when demanded for the performance of official duties by an immigration inspector, immigration guard, police officer, Maritime Safety Agency Officer, railway security officer, or member of any national or local body designated by Justice Ministry ordinance.'

Failure to carry the card is punishable by a fine of not more than ¥200,000. Failure to notify changes within the prescribed fourteen days can also carry a penalty of up to one year's imprisonment. This gives the victim a criminal record. By contrast, such an infringement of the Residents' Basic Register or the Domicile Register by Japanese nationals is subject to a correctional fine of ¥3,000 and does not constitute a criminal record. The Korean community's wish (which is related to the campaign for suffrage in local elections) is to be placed on the same basis as the Resident's Basic Register.

A court action in Osaka in 1988 resulted in some judicial criticism of the existing system. A Korean law student had been fined ¥8,000 by a summary court for not carrying the Alien Registration card. The fine was revoked, however, on appeal to the local higher court on the grounds that a penalty is not appropriate when the purpose is identification and this is served by other evidence such as a student's pass or driver's license. The Alien Registration system itself, however, was not ruled unconstitutional when applied for its specific purposes.

Although fingerprinting for permanent residents of all categories was abolished in the wake of the 1991 Memoire with South Korea, the long struggle leading up to it is part of the Korean community's collective memory and a factor in its continuing outlook. Apart from its association with implications of criminality one aspect that particularly rankled was that, in the vast majority of cases where a card bearer's identity might be in question, the fingerprint could not be used because the necessary experts and equipment were not on hand and in practice the photograph was used. The system was, then, essentially a means of harassment, of highlighting the Koreans' inferior, criminal-like status in Japan's hierarchy and of exerting pressure on them either to naturalize or repatriate themselves.

Although over the years many thousands of resident Koreans had been charged with various infringements of the Alien Registration Law, it was Han Chong-sok who triggered a systematic campaign to refuse fingerprinting in 1980. As he later recalled:

> I have given fingerprints any number of times but I came to reflect on my children and grandchildren having to continue being fingerprinted. I thought that, as I have nothing to speak of to leave my descendants, I might at least do something towards freeing them from this necessity. At

95

present in Japan the cries of 'internationalization' and 'international human rights' are being raised with vigor and I can't help feeling that the persistence of fingerprinting contradicts these. (Tanaka 1991)

He confessed to fear of being deported. His registration was, however, renewed, and he was formally charged in the Tokyo District Court early in 1983. This became the most prominent of a wave of 'fingerprint trials' which spread 'like a prairie fire' through the 1980s—especially after the major renewal date in 1985. Defendants of these trials were dealt with at various levels with varying degrees of severity and throughout the whole period legal action was taken against 3,670 fingerprint refusers.

Han provided the model for cases of this kind, defending his action on the grounds that fingerprinting infringed the spirit of the Constitution and conflicted with Japan's ratification of the Covenant on Human Rights. He also argued that resident Koreans were a settled part of Japanese society and merited different treatment from more transient aliens. In August 1984, he was convicted and fined ¥10,000. He appealed to the Tokyo High Court, which confirmed the sentence in August 1986. The case then went to the Supreme Court where the issue was evaded by an amnesty on the occasion of the Emperor's death in 1989. The amnesty covered all cases relating to fingerprinting, though this was the first time that an amnesty had been applied to a Supreme Court case. Han claimed that the Supreme Court had 'abandoned its mission as guardian of the Constitution' in dismissing the case without a verdict, since the acquittal he had hoped for would have ruled the fingerprinting rule unconstitutional.

He and others similarly affected then resorted to litigation to enable them to refuse the amnesty, so as to have their cases continued. This was, however, disallowed, although the ruling delivered on one such case at the Osaka District Court included the comment that 'the litigant's sentiments can be fully appreciated.' The legal situation also changed in that none of the litigants were now liable for fingerprinting. Prime Minister Nakasone, visiting South Korea in 1986, had announced that the law was being amended to require fingerprinting once only at the initial Alien Registration at age sixteen. There was also a considerable groundswell against fingerprinting in local administrations. Local assemblies, representing 70 percent of the Japanese population, adopted resolutions recommending fundamental changes to the law and many counter staff (such as those confronted by Yumi Lee) expressed support for placing resident Koreans on the same basis as the normal Residents' Basic Register.

Han Chong-sok vowed to continue the fight to free 16-year-olds from the fingerprinting requirement, but before his threatened case could come to court, the 1991 Memoire abolished all fingerprinting for permanent residents. Most of the other, often obnoxious, features of the Alien Registration system were left intact and remain a source of tension today.

In November 1994, a postscript to this issue was written in a Kyoto court. A friend of Yumi Lee's, Yun Ch'ang-yol, had been arrested in 1986 for refusing fingerprinting. He sued the Prefecture and government for wrongful arrest. He was able to demonstrate that there had been no fear of absconding or destruction of evidence (the only legal grounds for arrest in such a case) because he had given formal notice via his lawyer of his intent to contest the issue. He was finally awarded ¥400,000 damages.

8 The vote

The vote is generally regarded as 'the last hurdle' in securing civic rights for the Korean community. Prospects for voting rights at the local level have improved in recent years, but the situation remains complex. As ever, attitudes among the Koreans themselves are also divided.

Yumi Lee describes her feelings on this subject in detail:

> An announcement in a city bus said, 'Election day is coming up. Let's go to the election!' A number of posters of the candidates were put up all over town. This was a painful reminder that I am not considered a citizen. We do not have voting rights. Two centuries ago, America described this as 'taxation without representation.' I feel powerless at election time. Our voice is not reflected. We, as fully-fledged members of society, paying taxes imposed and performing the duty of labor do not have voting rights.
>
> Is there any other country than Japan that treats people of a former colony as complete foreigners without providing them with voting rights? I would call this apartheid. We are cut off from Japan's legislative system. There are only a few Japanese who know that we are not treated as citizens. We hear too often 'Is that true?'—even from teachers and university students. During one election campaign, a well known resident Korean university professor using his real name received a call from an election office. The caller asked, 'Mr. Kim, please take Mr. X into consideration for the next election.' He replied, 'I do not have voting rights.' The caller responded, 'You must be joking.'
>
> Mr. Lee Yong-hwa, who formed the Foreign Residents' Party, broke the silence about voting rights when he ran for election. The general public thought it was absurd. It took a fair amount of time before he was sufficiently understood. He had thrown a stone into the pond called the

general public, creating a rippling effect. The movement to obtain voting rights has been expanding constantly since 1993.

This movement has influenced those resident Koreans who had taken the lack of voting rights for granted. The real problem is this: the discriminated against become so numb that they do not recognize discrimination as such. Rights such as suffrage, equal employment, and equal accommodation should be legislated for. Resident Koreans do not have the right to decide policy or law because we do not have voting rights.

Ikuno Ward in Osaka, for instance, has a large concentration of Koreans. Twenty-five percent, or one in every four residents, are Korean. Because of lack of opportunity to participate in local administration, our voices cannot be reflected in the local government. A new exit to a subway was built far away from where the Koreans live, for example.

However, the movement to obtain suffrage has gained understanding from the administrations of a number of municipalities. On 4 December 1994, the dawn came for the civil rights movement for foreign residents. A thousand people participated in a gathering and parade. Mr. Lee Yong-hwa, who started the voting rights movement in Osaka, called the demonstration. Mr. Lee issues the Foreign Residents' Party newsletter *Nijiiro no Machi* (rainbow-colored society).

The demonstration was timed to coincide with the close of a lawsuit Lee had filed in the hope of advancing the cause. The unfavorable ruling, announced a few days later, advanced no material change. Lee, a lecturer at the Kansai University (a Japanese University in Osaka), had established a party with an entirely Korean membership. It was officially recognized as a party because there is no nationality restriction on political organizations. In 1991, Lee hoped to run candidates in the unified local elections, but his colleagues did not agree to this. In the same year, he pursued studies in Pyongyang, North Korea, and it was later rumored that he received instructions on his future activities from Chairman Kim Il-sung; this he ridiculed. While there, being a member of Soren and thus an 'overseas citizen,' he was entitled to vote in a local election. This was the first time in his life that he had ever had the opportunity to cast a vote. As often happens in socialist countries, there was only one candidate, so that the election amounted to a vote of confidence: as usual, the result was 100 percent.

In 1992, feeling that court action alone was inadequate to advance Koreans' rights in Japan, Lee decided to contest the Upper House election and, together with ten other party members from various areas, applied for candidature in the proportional representational division. Although their candidatures were rejected on the grounds that they lacked domicile registration certificates, they campaigned unofficially for votes (which would be treated as invalid) and signatures, as well as lodging deposits of ¥40 million with the Justice Ministry office. Other Koreans criticized this action on the grounds that it was better to concentrate on suffrage in local elections first rather than at the national level.

In an interview at the time, Lee was asked whether suffrage would promote assimilation among Koreans. He argued that the reverse was true, since the denial of foreign residents' rights promoted naturalization and assimilation. Concerning the disillusion of some radicals with parliamentary politics, with the implication that elections were futile and that it was pointless for Koreans to seek voting rights, he commented that the reason for apathy among Japanese voters was that they had not had to fight for democracy, but had it given to them 'like a dumpling falling into an open mouth' as the Japanese saying goes. He felt that Koreans should at least be given the chance to abstain from voting, which is also a political act.

To the argument that there were too few Koreans to affect politics appreciably, Lee pointed out that the Burakumin, numbering only 140,000 in Osaka Prefecture, had used their base there to achieve political successes. The local Korean population of 180,000 could be still more effective. To the objection that the suffrage would, on the contrary, split the community still further, with Soren affiliates voting for the Socialists and Mindan affiliates voting for the LDP, Komeito, or Democratic Socialists, Lee replied that such an outcome was better than an all-Korean bloc vote that would create a bad impression. He hoped that Korean representation would serve to protect minorities generally and also to promote the concept that the essence of democracy lies not in numbers but in the quality of debate.

Lee criticized the Mindan and Mintoren policy of giving priority to local suffrage on the grounds that local and national levels are inseparable. Blacks in the United States were given voting rights on both levels after the Civil War, while those in South Africa campaigned for both together. The same applied to Japanese women after World War II. In some European countries, resident foreigners have been restricted to local suffrage, but this was not the limit of their demands, only what governments were prepared to concede. In addition, resident Koreans prior to World War II had had the vote on both levels and were merely demanding the return of this right—not something new—so it was illogical to restrict it to only one level.

In the course of his campaign, Lee found a generally favorable reception among Korean residents and even recalled being cheered on by Korean *Yakuza* whom he encountered doing his rounds of the city.

Soon after the election he filed his suit with the Osaka District Court in the form of an appeal against an administrative decision on the grounds that the Constitution did not bar permanent residents from voting or standing for election. He did not expect outright success but hoped that, as in some previous cases, the ruling might include a criticism of legislation which could influence the Diet. This, however, was not forthcoming.

Another related lawsuit was meanwhile going on in the city of Fukui, on the Sea of Japan coast. It had been filed in May 1991 by four resident Koreans on the eve of Constitution Day with the aim of having their suffrage in local elections ruled constitutional. As their counsel put it: 'The guarantee of resident Koreans' human rights, with the establishment of shared living, signifies the real establishment of human rights and democracy in Japanese society. The securing of the suffrage is the indispensable precondition for the creation of a 'society of shared living.'

Argument was directed towards establishing that failure to register the plaintiffs on the electoral roll was illegal. Article 93 of the Constitution and five other relevant laws did not specify nationality for suffrage in local elections, and these took precedence over four laws which did so. In the first hearing in July 1991, one representative plaintiff was allowed to testify for only ten minutes, while the defense counsel representing the Justice Minister attempted to nullify the case on procedural grounds. These included the argument that the Electoral Control Committee could not be the subject of a national damages case and that in any case some error on its part would have to be established.

In the next hearing in November, no debate was allowed. An announcement was made that written arguments had been received which were adequate for immediate purposes. This naturally disappointed the assembled support group, who lodged complaints with the court and distributed protest leaflets. In the next hearing, once again only ten minutes were allowed to argue the validity of the case for restoring the suffrage rights of resident Koreans. In the court's final ruling, it was noted that in some countries local suffrage for aliens was allowed but that the matter had to be addressed by legislation.

Japanese supporters declined to be thanked and instead said that 'they would rather thank the plaintiffs for their efforts on behalf of a democratic and international Japan.' The Mindan, except for its Women's Section, was not actively involved and sent observers to court but not did not join the support group. Observers cynically commented that it was 'too busy with passport business.' The Soren remained aloof on the grounds that the suffrage would amount to a 'loss of ethnicity.' However, an Englishman, Alan Higgs, filed a comparable suit in Osaka and did not feel that his ethnicity in any way clashed with local suffrage based on residence.

From late 1993, some local government units began passing resolutions favoring local suffrage for resident aliens. In 1994, a Local Suffrage Acquisition Promotion Committee coordinated national efforts and based its campaign on the Covenant on Human Rights. By early 1995, over 100 local assemblies had passed resolutions in favor, including six prefectures and six major cities. A survey indicated that over half the 3,000 local units in Japan were likely to support local suffrage.

In February 1995, a ruling was obtained from the Supreme Court that the Constitution did not bar local suffrage for resident aliens and that it was only necessary to amend the Public Offices Election Law and the Local Government Law. Prime Minister Murayama then announced that his party would support such legislation aimed to take effect in time for the nationwide local elections four years away. Of his coalition partners, the LDP seemed to be responding favorably and the New Harbinger Party even more so. One of its branches had begun enrolling Koreans as members and was proposing a five-year residence qualification. The main opposition grouping, the New Frontier Party, organized a project team to formulate policy.

The Mindan-affiliated Young Korean Businessmen's Federation circulated a questionnaire to 759 members of the Diet and received 315 replies by the initial deadline. Of these, 276 (88 percent) favored local suffrage at once. Among these, 162 supported the right to stand for election as well. Most others indicated support at some future time and very few opposed, though presumably those not replying would not be in favor. By party breakdown, in the Lower House, 21 percent of the LDP, the most numerous party, replied with 74 percent of the Socialists and 67 percent of the Harbinger Party. The pattern was similar in the Upper House.

Overall, then, the prospects for ultimate success seem fair at this stage, though as in most issues the LDP seems likely to slow the pace of reform. The overall complexity of the political situation also discourages confident prediction.

Korean Diet members, pre-war and post-war

One Korean has been elected to each of the pre-war and post-war Diets but neither did much to advance Korean or reformist causes. Pre-war radicalism was severely discouraged, while the post-war requirement of naturalization implied a high degree of accommodation with the establishment.

The pre-war Dietman, Pak Ch'un-gum, came to Japan at the age of 16, a little before the annexation, and for some years worked partly as a laborer and partly as a seller of the popular Korean medicinal root ginseng. He moved about widely and seems to have been very resourceful, developing contacts alike among *Yakuza*, police, and Korean Government-General staff. This enabled him to found the Korean mutual aid society called the Soaikai in 1921. Although this was run by Koreans, it was essentially an instrument of indirect control by the authorities, and was used to break strikes and to suppress radical tendencies, so that Pak lost credibility in the community. When he stood for election in a Tokyo constituency in 1932, very few of the 1,200 Korean constituents there are said to have voted for him.

He did, however, receive strong support from his Government-General contacts, in both finance and publicity. They hoped to use him to promote their conciliatory policies as a counter to Korean aspirations for independence. In a working class area suffering in the Depression, his proposals for emigration of Japanese to Korea and Koreans to Manchukuo brought some support and involved clashes between his Soaikai members and supporters of socialist candidates. Pak also established a People's Council to channel support from small business. As a result, he was elected as an independent and gained the third highest vote in the Japanese style multimember constituency.

During his first term, to 1936, apart from the policies already noted, he agitated for an extension of the franchise to Korea. He coupled this with the introduction of voluntary military service. He failed in the 1936 election, however, because many changes had occurred, particularly in Government-General policies. A crackdown on electoral corruption also inhibited his maneuvers, so he began to cultivate a stronger base, supported by local businesses and a popular writer, and was re-elected in the snap election of early 1937. This election had been called by the military clique which hoped to win a majority for pro-military and right-wing parties, but the liberal and socialist parties decisively routed these opportunist elements.

Under the then constitution, Cabinets were appointed independently of Diet support, nominally by the Emperor but actually on the advice of the Senior Statesmen. Over the following years, the military and their bureaucratic allies gained complete control and launched wars in China and the Pacific. During this time, Pak pursued his proposals for Korea, advocating the establishment of a pro-Japanese regime in China. This was formed in 1940 with renegades from the Chinese Nationalists, though Pak did not wield any real influence among them.

He was sufficiently strong among the military to be included on their list of recommended candidates for the 1942 wartime election. He was, however, among the 20 percent who failed to be elected. He survived until 1973 in minor roles as a consultant to various groups.

The current ethnic Korean member of the Lower House is usually referred to by his naturalized name of Arai Shokei. He is a third generation Korean, born in Osaka in 1948 with the original name of Pak Kyong-jae. He was naturalized, together with his parents, in his last year in senior high school. He is described as being an introspective who cherishes the ideal of an egalitarian society.

He successfully entered the University of Tokyo, where he graduated in Economics and was also involved in the intense student agitation of the time. For some years, he did shift work at a blast furnace while studying for the Higher Civil Service examination, which he passed in 1973. He entered the Finance Ministry and, after holding executive posts in the taxation and banking offices, became the private secretary to the Minister in 1981. He is described as having demonstrated impressive social mobility at the cost of his ethnicity. However, he was widely admired and stood for election in 1983.

Although he received initial financial support from his mentor, the Minister, electoral costs were enormous as is well known in connection with the notorious scandals of recent decades. Since Arai was outside established political networks, he had to adopt 'guerrilla' electioneering tactics with strenuous efforts to develop personal links with the less committed circles in the Tokyo constituency he was to contest. In the New Year period, for example, he attended an average of 17 semi-formal gatherings per day. But his most keenly felt problem was racist tactics, such as attacks on his origin in public meetings or the word 'Chosen' being daubed on his posters. A candidate in a rival right wing faction of the LDP declared in a broadcast that Arai's loyalty would be in doubt in the event of a crisis in relations with Korea, North or South.

All these problems led to Arai's failure to be elected in 1983. He persisted nevertheless in building up a network in the small business sector and had 'acquired 250 supporters' associations' by the next election in 1986. On that occasion, he came a close second in the constituency and was elected as a member of the then dominant Nakasone faction. The South Korean press enthusiastically celebrated his success. On a visit to that country, he was asked where his first loyalty lay. He replied that it was to Japan, while his primary mission was directed to good relations with Korea and to Japan's internationalization generally.

He was subsequently re-elected despite such drawbacks as the Nakasone faction's involvement in scandals and the unpopularity of the LDP government's consumption tax. His future prospects are subject to the fluidity of the current situation and the effect of the reformed electoral system.

Part Three
CONFLICT BETWEEN THE TWO CULTURES

9 Marriage

Resident Koreans who wish to marry face several problems. Widely differing economic and educational levels exist in the Korean community, factors intensified under the abnormal conditions experienced by this group. A taboo exists on marriage within the same clan lineage, and, in addition, the persistent belief in the Chinese system of divination means that astrologically incompatible couples are discouraged from marrying—something that also occurs to some extent among Japanese.

In an ironic twist, sometimes a potentially suitable Korean couple, who both use Japanese aliases, remain unaware of each other's Korean ethnicity and both wrongly reject each other as a Japanese!

Soren affiliates, strongly affected by North Korean ideology, have tended to emphasize political acceptability in the choice of marriage partners. In some cases, however, this limitation has been countered by a stronger motivation to maintain at least some form of Korean identity. Women's organizations and Junior Business Associations arrange 'Cupid ceremonies' and 'bridal parties' to bring potential partners together, but a suitable marriage between Koreans is described as being 'as difficult as passing the entrance exam to a top-grade university.' (Kim Il-myon 1978) For obvious reasons, mixed marriages with Japanese suffer from a higher than average divorce rate. Marriages with Burakumin are said to be common but statistics on such cases are not available. Sometimes a Japanese husband avoids entering a Korean wife on his Domicile Register when he wants to keep her nationality concealed from his family.

A marginal type of case, common in the Osaka Family Court, involves de facto marriages by members of the sizable 'hidden population' of Koreans who have evaded Alien Registration. In order to avoid exposure when children are born, it is arranged for a friendly registered family to notify the birth as belonging to them. This deception can only be maintained until the child is of school age, when the family apply for 'confirmation of the absence of parental relationship.' What follows then depends on individual circumstances.

In the late 1980s, Min Kwan-shik and the Mindan carried out surveys and samplings of Mindan affiliates' attitudes to marriage. These give an indication of broad trends in that community. A breakdown between adults and tertiary and secondary students showed that 47 percent of the first group advocated inter-Korean marriage, as against 33 percent and 38 percent in the other groups. Those accepting marriage to Japanese came to 36 percent, 38 percent, and 52 percent respectively, but the tertiary group also contained a distinctive 24 percent who did not expect to find a Korean partner—an indication of the realities which are reflected in actual marriage statistics. A breakdown by age groups showed that 47 percent of those despairing of a Korean partner were in the 20-24 age group with about half that in the adjacent groups below and above. Others of course were less concerned. The largest group preferring a Korean partner was 40 percent in the 15-19 age group, perhaps reflecting a predominance of the ideal over realistic expectations. A breakdown between three linguistic groups classed as fluent in Korean, able to communicate and unable, rather naturally showed a descending preference for inter-Korean marriage of 75 percent, 56 percent, and 39 percent. A breakdown by educational levels among primary, junior secondary, senior secondary, and tertiary showed a preference for inter-Korean marriage among the last three groups of 65 percent, 45 percent, and 48 percent and acceptability of Japanese of 30 percent, 37 percent, and 37 percent respectively.

A survey of married Koreans showed that 75 percent of those married to Koreans preferred this choice while 35 percent of those married to Japanese replied that marriage to a Korean was preferable. But of the latter group, 49 percent replied that nationality was not crucial or less important than individual qualities, while only 18 percent of the former group did so. Another breakdown by age-groups, in this case by percentage over each age-group, showed an approximately linear decline in preference for inter-Korean marriage from the over 65 group to the 20-24 age group of 78 percent to 40 percent. Conversely, there was an increase in giving primacy to personal qualities from 3 percent to 37 percent and an expressed indifference to nationality from 6 percent to 15 percent. A comparison of married with unmarried subjects showed that 68 percent of the former preferred inter-Korean marriages as against 40 percent for the latter, who also showed a 48 percent indifference to nationality as opposed to 21 percent of the former.

A comparison by sex showed that 64 percent of males preferred inter-Korean marriage as against 60 percent of females, of whom also 30 percent were indifferent to nationality as against 24 percent for males. This agrees with the general trend in the Welfare Ministry's statistics for marriage, which show that the number of Korean women marrying Japanese have exceeded males since 1969. This means that the balance of males entering into partnerships would not register their marriage on their own Permanent Domiciles, which would be located in Korea, so that children would be entered on the wife's domicile and the marriage would not be recorded—a practice already noted.

These marriage statistics, of course, cover Koreans of all affiliations, so it would appear that the patterns described by the Mindan studies would have some relevance to Soren affiliates, although probably to a lesser degree.

Yumi Lee finds the issue of marriage a thorny problem:

> Alien registration, job hunting, and marriage are the three big events during life which make us confront our ethnicity. Marriage is often quite troublesome. I have never been in love with a Japanese man. With a Korean? No. With whom, then? I suppose it would be ideal to be in love with someone and marry just because you want to be with that person. Resident Koreans may be hesitant to go ahead and have love affairs. It is quite possible, and natural, for resident Koreans to fall in love with Japanese since we live in a Japanese environment. We often naturally start dating with someone from school or in the office. If we use an alias the person we are in love with would have no idea about our ethnicity. Sooner or later, however, we have to confess that we are Korean and are likely to hear the announcement that marriage is impossible. This is when many Koreans experience a bitter breakdown.
>
> I am from an average resident Korean family. Korean girls are especially protected and their parents commonly arrange their marriage. My parents are hoping for me to marry a Korean. If we marry a Japanese we are afraid of discrimination. My parents have seen that. Even if we love each other, when a problem arises, we are told 'You are just a Korean.'
>
> I met some Korean men through such family arrangements in my early twenties. Some were elite, such as doctors. I wanted to meet a Korean man with whom I could empathize. I was not unenthusiastic for an arranged marriage at all. Nevertheless, in traditional Korean society, after meeting a couple of times, you have to marry within a few months. Marriage is more a family-oriented matter than an individual one. After several such attempts, I decided it was not for me. I gave up arranged meetings with men. Korean parents sometimes entrust their daughters and sons to professional Korean match-makers. There is this feeling that marriage is the parents' responsibility.
>
> The reason why it did not work out with Korean men for me was the conservative Korean values to which most still cling. Men are believed to be valuable while women are worthless. Even today, those mothers who give birth to daughters are often looked down upon. It is a big problem in resident Korean society. I do not like this chauvinism. There are men who are very active to win rights for the Korean community who, at the same time, have a superior attitude towards women. I did not meet any with whom I could genuinely empathize. More than 80 percent

of resident Koreans marry Japanese. [Some of the Japanese married are probably naturalized Koreans but it is impossible to tell how many.] I think it is only natural, because we are born and raised in Japan. Those who are awakened to their Korean ethnicity hope either to marry Koreans or understanding Japanese. Those who are not awakened would naturally tend to marry a Japanese.

In any case, the parents on both sides would oppose the marriage for different reasons. Korean parents are worried that the marriage won't work. Japanese parents do not want to see their children marrying Koreans. In order to win approval from Japanese parents, Koreans often have to accept conditions, such as an agreement not to wear Korean folk dress for their wedding. This saves the Japanese parents from a feeling of 'shame.' A good friend of mine wanted to wear Korean dress for her marriage because it is a once in a lifetime event. However, she had to wear *shiromuku*, traditional Japanese dress.

I have five resident Korean women friends who are around thirty years old. They are independent, doing their own things like going abroad to study. We are well over the appropriate age for an arranged marriage. We joke about organizing a group for single Korean women. *Avant-garde* women are undesirable. Most Korean men do not understand us. Most want selfless and passive housewives. The resident Korean women who are able to be independent tend to stay single. They reject conservative Korean men. They are likely to be disappointed by Japanese society as well, and are hoping to go abroad.

Furthermore, the community is divided into two, which is a cruel tragedy for us. Although we are all Koreans, people split according to the organizations they belong to, the Soren or Mindan. This makes it difficult for couples when they belong to different organizations. The parents often block marriage between the two. On top of this, even when both belong to the same organization, their hometown (legal domicile in Korea) may matter. Sometimes I think it is hopeless because when a resident Korean wants to marry, s/he is screened out once by Japanese society and then by the Korean community.

My sister Ako once told me, when she was a student, that she deliberately avoided parties. The reason? She wanted to avoid falling in love with a Japanese man. Resident Korean women are not always free to have love affairs. Parents firmly protect their daughters, hoping they will marry a trustworthy Korean. Ako thought this was a natural thing to do. As she wants a quiet life, she chose a Korean who had been her friend for seven years. They seem to be happy now.

10 Accommodation

If public housing has been available in Japan to resident aliens following the ratification of the Covenant on Human Rights, private rented accommodation remains a difficult issue. Boarding houses often bear notices reading 'Not available for Koreans and Ryukyuans' so that unwanted tenants can even include some Japanese nationals. The conservative establishment regards the right of private contract as sacrosanct, so has resisted anti-discrimination legislation of the kind that in some countries bans such screening.

The barrier to public housing was not broken down without a campaign. Yumi Lee describes one such case in Kyoto which vividly illustrates the methods and psychology employed in her movement.

A Korean woman with a dependent daughter had won a draw for local public housing after trying for some years without her eligibility being questioned. She was now suddenly informed that such housing was not available to aliens.

> When they found out what had happened to Ms Chung, a citizen's group in Kyoto gathered at the City Hall. We were about fifteen and among them I found some familiar faces. Some were volunteer teachers for the 'Mother's School' [a school for illiterate older women where Yumi Lee taught], while others were members of a group aiming to improve the residential environment in southern Kyoto, the area where the Korean population is concentrated.
>
> We started to distribute flyers around eight o'clock to City Hall employees. Then we swarmed into the office. We started to shout out: 'Stop discrimination!' 'Housing discrimination is unjust!' I was taken aback by this strategy. It was nothing like peaceful negotiation. It was extremely powerful and I didn't like it very much. Demonstrators also used a loudspeaker. 'Get the director' 'Talk!' The language used was also rough, like gangsters. Later I found out this was an effective strat-

egy, intentionally adopted. One of the members explained: 'If we are polite, the Japanese would say "We will think about it" or "We will take it into consideration." This is equivalent to "We won't do anything!"' These people had experience and knew what they were doing. When we are polite and soft, Japanese also play polite and soft. The first thing to do is to show that we are serious. To do so, we needed to show a threatening attitude. Then the Japanese would realize that the issue is important.

Finally City Hall promised us that we would meet the director and another person. They invited us into the conference room. The two bureaucrats merely repeated typical responses: 'It is because of the circumstances we are in,' 'we will take it into consideration,' etc., etc., avoiding confrontation. Each of us appealed in turn. 'How could you treat us so badly without knowing the reason why Koreans are in Japan?' I appealed loudly. In doing so, I started to realize the purpose of using a loud voice because of their response. They only show their face as an administrative body. We continued: 'Can't you see the issue on a more humanitarian basis?' One demonstrator pointed out that Kyoto's slogan as an international and humanitarian city read 'Protect Human Rights. Stop Discrimination.' It should read 'Protect discrimination. Dismiss human rights,' he said.

A few weeks after our protest, qualifications for applicants for public housing changed. Now it read: 'Aliens with permanent residence rights accepted.' And Ms Chung was accepted for public housing.

Cases like this may now be in the past, but Yumi Lee also has an example of the more intractable problem of private accommodation. It relates to her sister Ako's marriage to a fellow Korean.

Before their marriage, they went off to housing agencies to find new living quarters. When they were visiting one agency, the man showed them lists of newly built apartments especially for newly wed couples. They began excitedly comparing the apartments. But when the agent found they were Koreans, he began to take the lists away, saying 'This is not available, neither is this one . . . .' They had to go elsewhere to find a place to live. But it was the same everywhere. They were looking for a bright future together, but the wedding date was getting closer and closer, and they were worn out. One agent guaranteed that he would find a place 'which accepts even resident Koreans.' He came up with an apartment facing a national road with heavy traffic. The room was damp and the rent high. 'Ordinary Japanese' would not choose this. Now they are living in that apartment, but still hoping that they can find a better place closer to their ideal.

In another case, a Japanese was unable to obtain accommodation because he planned to marry a Korean. He became romantically attached to a girl active in the youth section of the Mindan. After a year's association, they explored the possibility of marriage. She had been brought up by her grandparents, and although her grandmother had no objection to the idea, her grandfather was opposed because he had been a military conscript and suffered for it. He told his grand-daughter's proposed partner that he had nothing against him personally, 'only the Japanese label attached to him.'

The Japanese man's parents also opposed the match, pleading the embarrassment it would cause the relatives and telling him that if he persisted he would have to be removed from the domicile register. It later turned out that they were testing his resolve. He decided to leave home and find separate quarters, but every agent he consulted demanded that he present not only his own domicile registration but also his prospective wife's. On being told she had only Alien Registration, he was told that 'it would be appreciated if he desisted.' This is described as having happened at 'hundreds of agencies.' (Kyoto-shi Kokusai Koryu Kyokai 1994)

Yumi Lee has also failed to get accommodation for herself in Kyoto when she tried to leave home and rent an apartment. When she makes inquiries over the phone, she is rejected as soon as she mentions her Korean name 'Lee.' A typical experience occurred when she telephoned a real estate agent in response to an apartment ad in the newspaper. 'The real estate agent said the apartment was vacant and eagerly tried to get me to make an appointment to see it. When I told him my name, the apartment was no longer available.' When she goes around Kyoto to talk to agents, they usually say that landlords refuse to rent to non-Japanese tenants because of language difficulties and exotic cooking. This is absurd in her case as Japanese is her native language and she only occasionally cooks in Korean style, but all agents insist that landlords are inflexible and won't make any exceptions. (Research/Action Institute for Koreans in Japan, *Japan's Subtle Apartheid* 1990)

Faced with the accommodation problem the Koreans have once again taken to the courts. (The Korean faith in the Japanese judicial system seems limitless and by and large has not been misplaced.) The first litigation was in Osaka in 1989. Pae Kon-il had hoped to acquire a more spacious home where his son would have room to study properly. On finding a suitable place, he was told by the agent that Japanese nationality was required. A suggestion to put the house in his Japanese wife's name was refused. Pae then sued the landlord, the agent, and the Osaka Prefecture in the Osaka District Court. He also gathered 10,000 signatures to support his case which dragged on for years, over 23 sessions. His counsel, in the final summing up, declared that a society where this could happen could not be described as truly international:

113

The plaintiff, in the course of the hearing, has demonstrated the reality of ethnic discrimination perpetuated in the name of freedom of contract and how, by such abuse of freedom and by administrative remissness, resident Koreans, including the plaintiff, have been made to sense an insult to their humanity.

The case was substantially successful, since it was judged that, despite contractual negotiation having progressed to a certain stage, the landlord had refused to conclude the contract without rational cause. Pae was awarded ¥267,000 damages, although the agent and the Prefecture were absolved of responsibility. He hoped, however, that the result of the case would bring an improvement in public attitudes. (Min 1994)

11 The Utoro mass eviction case

The largest case involving Korean occupancy rights was still unresolved at the time of writing. It involved the attempted eviction in 1988 of an entire Korean neighborhood from land that they had occupied since the end of World War II. Although the resident Koreans had not acquired formal title to the land, the circumstances which had led to their residence and certain complex maneuvers surrounding the eviction order disposed the legal authorities, when it came before them, to take a conciliatory approach.

The area is included in the City of Uji in Kyoto Prefecture, only twenty minutes by train from Kyoto Central Station. It is called Utoro, a name so unusual that it is sometimes assumed to be Korean, especially as, uniquely among place names, no Chinese characters are used for it, but it is apparently local dialect meaning 'a hollow.' It covers 21,000 square meters and comprises over 80 households with a population of nearly 400. It is described as a microcosm of Korean community problems stemming from the War. It was originally settled by Korean laborers who were assembled to work on a military airfield being constructed by a state controlled aeronautical corporation in the later stages of the War. The laborers, numbering 1,300 at the peak of construction, were not part of the forced draft system but recruited by more normal procedures. The airfield was unfinished when the War ended, and the laborers abandoned to their own devices. Those who did not return to Korea or find other alternatives stayed on in the very crude quarters built to house laborers in such cases. They survived by the precarious means sketched earlier. In time, as with other Korean communities, they achieved a tolerable existence and Utoro became home to them.

Meanwhile, the area had been acquired by the Nissan Chassis Company which in the 1960s held occasional negotiations with the settlers, sometimes through the Soren, about the status of the land and possible arrangement for the settlers to purchase it or to resettle elsewhere. These were, however, inconclusive. When the settlers applied to Uji City to be connected to the public water supply because they had access only to brackish wells, the city would not comply without agreement from Nissan. Nissan refused on the grounds that this would confirm the settlers' occupancy. In 1984 and 1985, Nissan made a concrete offer to the head of the Area Council, Ho Ch'ang-gu, usually known as Hirayama Masuo, for the purchase of the land. Two residents' meetings to consider this failed to reach any decision.

By 1986, agitation for a better water supply was growing intense. Nissan proposed a plan to settle both the land ownership and the water issue. The land would be sold to a company which Hirayama would set up to resell land to the residents in individual lots. Water and road construction costs would be apportioned according to the area of each lot. With Hirayama's agreement to this scheme, Nissan advised Uji City in 1987 that they consented to the water supply, which went ahead, much to the delight of the residents who remained ignorant of the real reason for it. At the same time, a contract of sale to Hirayama was concluded. The two existing copies show discrepant amounts of ¥400 million and ¥300 million. Hirayama then made a deposit of ¥50 million and established a company called Western Japan Development, with himself as a director, to which he resold the land for ¥445 million. Concealing all this, he petitioned residents inquiring whether they wished to purchase land by lots. No agreement was reached, and it was only in mid-1988 that the residents, alerted by rumors, checked land registration records and discovered the truth. Hirayama resigned his directorship of the company later in the year and disappeared.

The residents formed a Countermeasures Committee and sought legal advice. At the end of the year, however, they received unconditional eviction notices by post from the new board of Western Japan Development. They ignored the eviction notices, and the company filed a lawsuit against them in the Kyoto District Court. In February 1989, demolition workers approached the site. The residents physically repulsed them. In March, a more widely based support group called the Association to Protect Utoro was formed at the Kyoto Lawyers' Hall, with an initial membership of 70 and an attendance of 200 including housewives, clergymen, and public employees. Soon afterwards a demonstration including about 700 persons was held at Nissan Chassis' Kyoto Works and negotiations were attempted through the Uji City office. The residents demanded that, since Nissan had intended to sell them the land, the company should buy it back and deal directly with them. A larger demonstration was later held at the Nissan Corporation's head office in Tokyo. The corporation maintained, however, that it had no further responsibility for the land.

Court hearings began in March. The residents based their case partly on their long occupancy and development of Utoro, and partly on the claim that they were owed some form of compensation to atone for both their wartime treatment and the administration's subsequent neglect of any rational settlement. The case was stated at the opening meeting of the Association to Protect Utoro by Professor Emeritus Higuchi Kin'ichi as follows:

> The Koreans have not yet been compensated for the aggressive war and colonial control that robbed them of their language, names, and lives. It is the proper role of Japanese to apologize for these crimes and atone for them. The Utoro question is one that would not have arisen but for Japan's pre-war aggression and colonial control in Korea. It would not have arisen if the administration had taken due responsibility for the liquidation of this history of aggression and control.

The underhand procedure adopted in selling the land without consulting the residents was also condemned. This stand was strengthened when it was found that Hirayama's copy of the contract, tendered by Western Japan Development, showed a price of ¥400 million as against ¥300 million in that obtained from Nissan. This aspect could not be fully pursued because of Hirayama's disappearance. (Asahi Shimbunsha 1992)

From November 1991 to June 1992, nine closed sessions were held on the judge's initiative in an attempt to reach a compromise price for the sale of the land to the residents. Residents contested the figures suggested by Western Japan Development on the grounds that the bubble economy had burst. A duly incorporated Block Council replaced the Countermeasures Committee and was empowered to handle the collective interests of the settlement. With the breakdown of negotiations on the sale price, the court proceedings returned to the customary pattern of long-winded and protracted legal arguments.

Meanwhile, efforts were made to extend the campaign to a broad national and international level. In June 1990, a group of Socialist Party members visited Utoro. This led to questions raised in a House of Representatives Legal Committee session. The Land Use section head of the Land Agency stated that no notice of the sale of the land had been received, suggesting an infringement of the Land Use Planning Law. When the Socialist members pressed the Justice Minister for his opinion on Nissan's irresponsible attitude to the residents' livelihood and on national responsibility for the airfield project which had created Utoro, the Minister declined to comment—on the grounds that the matter was *sub judice*.

An international dimension was introduced in August, on the 45th anniversary of the end of the War, by an International Peace Forum in Utoro, held in Uji. It was attended by Korean atomic bomb victims, and an American editor and translator named Robert Ricketts, who had been convicted for his refusal to be fingerprinted. There was also a delegation from Germany invited by a local woman, Tagawa Akiko, who had earlier visited Germany in a delegation of the Japanese-German Peace Forum. They drew a parallel between Nissan and Volkswagen, which had employed conscripted Polish and Russian labor during the War but was now commissioning research on the issue, to be published the following year. They concluded that, although the fall of the Berlin Wall was expected to promote peace, 'what must be broken is not a visible wall but the walls within us of racism, hostility to other nationalities, and habitual discrimination.' Ricketts also elaborated his views at the Forum on the faults of Occupation policy, claiming that the obsession with fighting Communism had led to the neglect of effective social reform.

Yumi Lee quotes her diary:

> We received four guests from Germany who came for the International Peace Forum in Utoro tomorrow. Japan and Germany have similar pasts; nevertheless the way each country has handled the issues differs dramatically. People in Utoro still suffer, forty-five years after World War II. What a contrast! In Germany even private business corporations have compensated the victims.
>
> I accompanied these German guests when they visited the mayor of Uji. They asked the mayor directly, as Westerners usually do, about responsibility for the Utoro issue. The Mayor was equivocal and flustered. Ironically, there is a monument in front of the Uji City Hall that reads: 'Uji city is a city of peace.'

The following spring a return visit to Germany was made by Ms Kang Hye-jong, a Korean who had been born in Switzerland. She joined the annual Japanese-German Peace Forum held at Humboldt University on the anniversary of peace in Europe.

Later in the year, there was a visit by a representative of the substantial Korean population in Kazakhstan, Gherman Kim, a historian with that Republic's Academy of Sciences. He had been studying Korean in Seoul as there is little knowledge of the language in his community. Kazakhstan's Korean community number about half a million, a legacy of the mass transportation of Korean settlers from Siberia's Maritime Province under Stalin's regime. Ironically, the Stalinist authorities had been afraid that they would help Japan undermine Soviet defenses in the event of war, though the sole reason for their presence was their desire to escape Japanese control. Amid the multiethnic population of Kazakhstan, Kim said, the Korean community had a high status. It included lawyers, academics, and government ministers. There is even a Korean newspaper in Kazakhstan, the *Koryo Daily*.

In September 1991, Yumi Lee began a three-month speaking tour of the United States to publicize the Utoro Case and, through it, a whole range of Korean issues in Japan. She had made American contacts at a symposium in Kyoto in 1990 on the Korean question and received invitations to speak at both Harvard and Yale. She lectured at the University of Massachusetts, the Queens Korean Association, Columbia University, civic groups, the Japanese

Women's Association at Amherst, and the New York Japanese-American Association for the Elimination of Racial Discrimination, as well as at the Long Island branch of the National Organization for Women. She distributed her pamphlet *Who has Heard Japan-born Koreans' Voice?* Her account of the speaking tour describes how her slides of Utoro had a strong impact through their concrete representation of the Korean's plight. She was also interviewed on television.

On her return to Japan, she was much in demand for lectures on her American experiences. She accepted another invitation to the United States in the following February. Then she attended the annual Korean-American Conference and reported that she was 'overwhelmed again by the power of Koreans in America.' For the rest of the year, she was largely occupied by the comfort women issue. In February 1993, she attended a press conference in Tokyo at the Foreign Correspondents' Club with the Utoro support group. They were planning a one-page opinion ad in the *New York Times*. The conference was attended by representatives of CNN, *Time,* the *New York Times,* and *Newsweek,* all of whom were raising the Utoro issue to an international level. The opinion ad was published on 1 March with the aid of the Kyoto branch of the Public Media Center. It is described as receiving a 'vast feedback,' particularly from the Korean community. Yumi was interviewed live by a Los Angeles radio station who wanted her to speak in her 'broken Korean for Korean listeners.' She was also interviewed by the print media.

In April 1991, Chimoto Hideki, an associate professor at Tsukuba University, published an article in the *Kyoto Shimbun* describing the Utoro case as the government's 'third crime,' following colonization and refusal of war compensation. He was concerned that similar attitudes to those of the past were now being applied to the substantial number of laborers of other Asian nationalities now flooding into Japan in numbers comparable to the established Korean community. He suggested that Japanese should study Ryukyan and Ainu cultures to realize that indigenous Japanese society already has a multiracial component and as a means of extending this realization to accommodate Koreans, Chinese, Filipinos, and others.

12 Work

Discrimination in hiring and employment keeps many Koreans resident in Japan from pursuing the careers of their choice. Resident Koreans face both de facto and de jure discrimination, and in at least one anecdotal case, job discrimination led to a young woman's suicide. Yumi Lee gives some personal experience of the problems facing resident Koreans in the vocational field:

> Before entering college I thought about my future again and again. I came to the conclusion that I wanted to be a Physical Education teacher since I loved sports. I chose my target college to be Osaka Physical Education University. I went to my elder sister to talk about it. She said, 'A Korean cannot be a teacher.' I remember reading in Malcolm X's biography that he was told to give up becoming a lawyer. In 1982, in Japan, I was told to give up becoming a teacher.

Yumi Lee was not the only one whose career ambitions were doomed. Ten years later she heard of the tragic outcome of a similar case from a teacher at St. Agnes' College, a private school Yumi Lee had attended:

> The teacher told me the following: 'A girl in my class committed suicide last year. Her major was nursery studies. One night she stayed in an inn where she had been with her family years before. The next day she jumped off a cliff. The college treated it as the mere suicide of an insignificant student. I believed there must be some reason behind it. I investigated!'
>
> The girl who committed suicide was a Korean. So the teacher, Ms Tomeoka, started investigations and found the girl's journal. She had written that she wanted to be a kindergarten teacher. But a Korean could not do that. When confronted with the reality, she became depressed and lost hope for the future. Ms Tomeoka communicated her findings to the

120

college and insisted on its significance so that they should investigate. The college, afraid of being stuck with the issue, stubbornly treated it as just 'a suicide of a student.'

Job opportunities for Koreans in this field became available after the 1991 Memoire, though career prospects were still limited. One reason quoted as to why Koreans were thought unsuitable to teach Japanese children—and something revealing of Japanese psychology—was that 'Koreans cannot understand the pathos that Japanese feel when they view the cherry blossoms.' This does not refer simply to aesthetic appreciation but to the sense of evanescence and tragedy underlying beauty which has been such a major theme in Japanese culture, as for instance in Noh drama. The idea was that such subtle nuances could only be conveyed to later generations by Japanese themselves, since Koreans were too direct or forthright. However, as one Korean comments, some Japanese do not appreciate this pathos, while some Koreans may.

Yumi Lee has more to say on the subject of careers:

> I did not want to take up a job which, because I am a Korean woman, requires only running routine errands and ordinary office work. I wanted something that needed me and my ability in an international setting. The job I had in mind was a stewardess. In Asia, a flight attendant is still thought to be an attractive way of living. We had an employment center in our school. Without knowing how blatant the discrimination against Koreans was, I went to it and inquired about a stewardess position at Japan Air Lines. I mentioned that I was a resident Korean. Later, when I went back to the center, I was told: 'It looks impossible. There is no previous example of hiring Koreans.' At the Japan Tourist Bureau, I was told the same thing.

Yumi Lee persisted and was eventually employed for a time by Korean Air Lines but subsequently has held only part-time positions in private or extracurricular teaching, translating, or the like. She takes up the story:

> I saw an ad in the newspaper looking for guide interpreters who could work for the International Textile Fair. By this time I knew that I, as a Korean, was disadvantaged in employment. Nevertheless, I applied for the position, hoping my English would win through. The interviewers had seemed to be impressed with my English and my background of having worked as a flight attendant. When I was accepted for the position, I was told: 'In principle we do not accept Koreans. However, we decided to make an exception especially for you.'

Usually we use a standard resume when applying for a position. One of the items you have to fill in is the legal domicile. If you are a Japanese national, you put the name of the hometown where your family registry is. But because we are not registered in a Japanese family registry, we have to write our nationality. I have been writing 'Korean.' Once I wrote 'Kyoto' (my hometown) instead of 'Korean' when I badly wanted to work in a bakery as a part-timer. It was a lie. I worked for that bakery for a while, under my Japanese alias, Uno. However, when you are applying for a full-time job, it is a different story. The employer will invariably request a certificate of domicile registration, which I do not have.

Kim Il-myon gives another vivid account of one woman's employment vicissitudes. (*Chosenjin ga naze* 1978) She had attended a municipal junior high school in Kobe, where she usually topped the class. Partly because of this and partly because one-third of the pupils were Korean (not to mention a large number of Burakumin), she was elected every year to the head of the class committee. However, when she got to senior high, the classes were overwhelmingly Japanese. She felt isolated and concealed her Korean origins.

Around graduation time, with her teacher's encouragement, she took a number of employment examinations but kept failing until she realized that her only hope was to apply for positions where a legal domicile certificate was not required. As a result, she was accepted into an insurance company, where she completed the induction course and worked for about a week. Then the personnel section demanded her domicile certificate. When she revealed that she did not have one, she was fired on the spot. As she tidied her desk before leaving, her workmates, not knowing the reason for her sudden dismissal, suggested that the employees' union might negotiate to have her stay on. However, since she did not want her Korean origins to be known, she declined their offer.

She next found work with a shipping company which did not raise the matter of a domicile certificate, but since she was with the counter staff handling passenger inquiries, she was constantly on guard for fear that some acquaintance would notice and expose her. One lunch-break, after she had been working there for six months, a workmate told her that some Korean illegal immigrants had just been caught nearby and suggested that they go and look. As she watched the 20 pitiful figures being taken from their flimsy craft and lined up in front of the Maritime Safety Agency office, she experienced an awakening. She felt ashamed at her efforts to pass as a Japanese.

After this she lost interest in succeeding at her work. She longed only to associate with Koreans. Her opportunity to make real contact with her heritage came through an encounter with a member of the Soren's Youth League, who took her to a Korean youth festival on scenic Mt Rokko behind Kobe. Here girls her own age were performing dances in Korean costume. She left the shipping company, telling her workmates that she was a Korean and for a time worked with her mother in a rubber factory. Finally, she became a full-time activist with the Youth League at half the pay she had received at the factory. She had no ideology other than wishing to serve the Korean community. She remarked that if someone from the Mindan had come at the critical time, she would probably have gone with them instead.

To sum up, private employment tends to be restricted to medium or small scale enterprises. For public or semi-public employment, the situation in local government is the same as for teaching. The nationality qualification was removed for the Japanese Telecommunications Corporation in 1978; for full professorships in state universities in 1982, though associate professorships had been available earlier; for postal employees in 1984 after a campaign originating in Osaka the previous year; and for nursing on a nationwide basis in 1986 after another such campaign.

In other professions, Koreans have figured in the medical field since before the war. The nationality requirement was relaxed for lawyers in 1977 as the result of another major campaign. The central figure in this, Kim Kyong-duk, had graduated in the Law faculty of the top-ranking Waseda Private University, long associated with liberalism and high quality journalism. He had hoped for a career in journalism but found that his nationality prevented this. He therefore turned to law and passed the Justice Ministry's judicial examination, a very stiff barrier in which only one in 60 candidates succeed. In order to become a lawyer, however, he had to complete a two-year traineeship at the Judicial Research and Training Institute. When he applied for this to the Supreme Court, he was informed that he could only be admitted if he agreed to be naturalized. The law itself did not exclude lawyers of foreign nationality, but the traineeship was regarded as a form of government employment from which aliens are excluded.

Some ethnic Koreans and Taiwanese had already accepted this condition and completed the traineeship, but Kim, influenced by the early 1970s awakening of the Korean community surrounding the Hitachi Case, believed that this would conflict with his major aim of protecting the interests of the Korean community who could hardly feel confidence in him if he naturalized. So he addressed an eloquent petition to the Supreme Court requesting that the condition be waived.

> From childhood I resented having been born as a Korean and endeavored to eliminate everything Korean from me. Through the social and professional discrimination I experienced after my university graduation I came to wonder what I could achieve that would be most effective for the elimination of discrimination against Koreans and for the democratization of Japan; how I could compensate for the void of

the past twenty-three years when I had devoted myself to evading the discrimination of Japanese society, and how I could turn to account my studies in the Faculty of Law. I concluded that this would mean passing the judicial examination, becoming a judicial trainee, and a Korean lawyer. So for four years I studied for the examination, supporting myself by part-time work, and this year I qualified.

At this point I cannot heedlessly apply for naturalization. This would mean forfeiting the very basis of my ambition to become a lawyer.

He enlisted the help of a group of lawyers and academics including Professor Tanaka Hiroshi. This group presented a submission to the Supreme Court carefully analyzing the relevant legislation. Aliens were not excluded from the judicial examination, while a ruling was also found that foreign lawyers could only practice if they gained Japanese qualifications. It was illogical to exclude them from the training. The National Bar Association also submitted a favorable opinion.

Early in 1977, after three months' deliberation, the Supreme Court admitted Kim to the Institute. He later became a prominent figure in Korean legal causes. The court described his admission as a special case, without elaborating on the reasons. In time, however, the rules for admission were amended so that the exclusion of aliens was qualified by 'except in cases deemed appropriate by the Supreme Court.' (Tanaka 1991) In practice, suitably qualified candidates came to be admitted regularly. By 1993, about 50 lawyers of Korean extraction were practicing and a few of these had been naturalized.

Because they face difficult employment conditions, it is natural that a large part of the Korean community operate their own businesses. These are usually small-scale and precarious, though fortunately the generally buoyant Japanese economy has helped them survive and occasionally prosper. One survey introduces the topic in the following terms.

The scale (and type) of businessmen's operations covers a wide range, from company enterprises such as joint-stock and limited companies, to independent businesses and private concerns. Some employ hundreds of people, while some are individual or family operations. Among Korean businesses, a few are manufacturers with a staff of hundreds or enterprises which rate well on the stock exchange, while many are very small, down to tiny snack-bars able to seat only a handful of people. (O Kyu-sang 1992)

A survey of Korean businesses in the two main concentrations of Osaka and Tokyo show contrasting patterns. In Osaka, 46 percent were in manufacturing (plastic, metalwork, machinery and fittings, spinning, footwear), 19 percent in sales (including wholesale recycling and restaurants), 16 percent in service industries (games and entertainment, with a disproportionately large turnover), and the rest in construction, real estate, money lending, insurance agencies, motor transport, and bank agencies.

In Tokyo, 30 percent were in service industries (*pachinko*, hotels, saunas, tax agents, medical), 28 percent in sales (wholesale recycling, restaurants and cafes, night clubs), 22 percent in manufacturing, while the rest were much the same as in Osaka. (Min 1994) Many of the community, as noted earlier in passing, are employed in small-scale business either Japanese or Korean owned, sometimes under sweat-shop or piece-work conditions. One such case mentioned incidentally for having made a disproportionately large contribution to the DPRK via the Soren was a widow working as a subcontractor of a small retail factory. She was working on a sewing machine all day, with each sewn item yielding a marginal gain of only a couple of hundred yen. Such cases would probably predominate among the unregistered 'hidden population' for whom figures are not available.

Both the Soren and the Mindan have networks of business associations, credit unions, and insurance. As already noted, Soren affiliates make a substantial contribution to the North Korean economy. Mindan-affiliated contributions to the South are less significant or needed, though occasionally noted, as in the case of assistance to the Seoul Olympic Games. Some elements in the community resented this, especially those who are pro-North and also the younger generation, who identify less with South Korea. According to Ryang (1996), there are 28 companies associated with the Soren, including the Kumgang Insurance Co. and Choshin Bank, which controls 38 credit unions throughout the country. The Mindan counterpart, Kanshin, controls 35, with a comparable volume of business. Some Koreans apparently use both. Regarding insurance, Mindan is described as combining with Toho Life Insurance.

Koreans are limited in job choices in less direct ways. Golf clubs represent an important social adjunct of Japanese business life. There are approximately 2,000 of these in Japan, ranked hierarchically, in which the highest membership fee is ¥300 million. In many cases membership is restricted to those of Japanese nationality. In 1988, a survey of 257 clubs in the Kanto region, centered on Tokyo, revealed that 57 percent had a nationality restriction and 86 percent required sponsorship by existing members. One representative case required the following documents for an application for membership: domicile registration certificate, three photographs, guarantee, personal history, seal sample, and signed postcard. Nationality was limited to Japanese, females were limited to a total of 140, age had to be over 35, and an introduction was required from two members, one to be of at least five years' standing. The reason for requiring the domicile certificate, as in the case of employment, was to exclude Koreans using Japanese names.

In 1989, when the Golden Golf Club in Shimonoseki, a city with a sizable Korean community at the Western tip of Honshu, advertised for members but no non-Japanese, it was attacked by the local Korea-Japan Friendship Association. This was the first assault on the formidable barriers of ethnic discrimination in Japan's golfing world, and it was not to be the last.

In 1994, a second-generation Korean in a satellite town east of Tokyo resorted to litigation. He was president of a paint company, which became a corporate member of a golf club. Since this club excluded non-Japanese, membership was registered in the name of a branch head and the company president was allowed to take his place in the capacity of 'playing member.' Later, when the club invited playing members to become registered members, his application was refused. He sued for a solatium in the Tokyo District Court. The club argued that it was a private organization, and that even where there are no nationality clauses, as in Western countries, members reserve the right of veto on new admissions.

In early 1995, there was a more positive result. The Court found in favor of the plaintiff on the grounds that the club's action infringed Article 14 of the Constitution, specifying equality under the law. He was awarded membership (pending application) and a ¥300,000 solatium.

This was a historic victory—but there is still a long way to go. To get a general idea of the policies of golf clubs, a Mindan-affiliated consultative body recently polled all 1,794 golf clubs listed in a public guidebook on the nationality question. Of the 821 which replied, 170 had a nationality clause, though 20 of these planned to drop it. Reasons given for it ran: 'There is a strong consciousness of being an essentially Japanese gathering of intimates and there is a general mood in the club that foreigners are not welcome.' Another said: 'One feels awkward with foreigners around.' This is true, it seems, if foreigners can only be identified by their lack of a domicile registration certificate.

13 Violence and the school system

The general level of violence in Japan is exceptionally low compared to other industrialized countries for a variety of reasons. These include the stability of the family system and social discipline generally, the country's economic prosperity, and effective firearms control. The waves of violence against Koreans that have occurred from time to time have then been all the more conspicuous. The media, by highlighting crises of this kind, have certainly not helped overall, though some have carried protests against the violence.

The most disturbing examples are attacks on students attending ethnic schools, particularly girls who are easily identified by their Korean costume (*chima-chogori*). A sympathetic Japanese has protested in the following verse:

The Words that cut our Hearts
Inogawa Oki (1990)
(translated by Kawashima Megumi)

I am on the way to school,
'Go home!' I hear. [i.e. back to Korea]
I am walking on the street.
'Go home!' I hear.
I am on the train,
'Go home!' 'Go home!' 'Drop dead!'
Words transform into stones,
They hit a boy's back.
Words become a cleaver,
They tear through chima-chogori girls are wearing.
Despite all that, the Prime Minister of this country says: [PM Kaifu 1989]
'I did not bully them'—sitting deep on a soft big chair.

Parents of these boys and girls,

127

Targeted by the officials of this country,
Dragged away from and forced to leave the land
Where they somehow made their living,
Traveled across the straits.
Some were taken straight from the field,
No time even to change their peasant dress.
Some were still holding chopsticks.
They were all loaded onto the truck as cattle,
No time to say good-bye
And transported by force to this country.

Fifty years have passed since those days.
The history of aggression was pressed into darkness,
Behind the scenes.
The shape of racial discrimination came under bright lights, yet—
No word of apology.
The nation reviles us: 'Go home!'
The Minister turns his face aside,
'Bullying is a common problem in all schools in Japan.'

A female freelance journalist, Nishino Rumiko, who belongs to the Association for War Research and who has published a volume of exhaustive studies on the comfort women question, wrote in 1994 about the violence against Korean girls:

> Assault and verbal abuse against Korean girls and students have increased. It started just when Japanese public opinion was becoming more favorable in recent years to recognizing Japan's war responsibilities. Assault on the girls seems to be intended to shift public opinion. It is utterly unforgivable. Several years ago, similar incidents happened. Girls wearing *chima-chogori* were attacked. I cannot forget what one of the girls assaulted said: 'I will not take off my *chima-chogori* since it symbolizes Korean ethnic pride.' A just settlement of Japan's war compensation is needed, not only for its own sake but also to stop girls being assaulted and threatened. I am angry that girls are repeatedly targeted when any friction arises between Korea and Japan. A series of incidents involving Soren alarmed many resident Koreans. I believe this also alarmed many Japanese as a threat to democracy.
>
> I believe the only way Japan can cohabit with other Asian countries is to take responsibility for the war. Japan was an aggressor. By making our role as the aggressor clear, the manipulation of public opinion by the authorities will be exposed. The authorities try to promote as a 'kind of national sentiment' the image of a fearsome North Korea. Those who

are persuaded by this abuse Korean children and schoolgirls. It is frightening because it looks as if Japan is going backwards the way it came. Japanese have to recognize that all the issues, Korean human rights, comfort women, and forced laborers, stem from the same root. It is for Japan to settle the problem by taking action. Japan has to maintain a social atmosphere so that girls in Korean folk dress can commute without fear, but with a smile.

The first wave of violent attacks was a reaction against the long and widespread campaign against the Normalization Treaty of 1965 waged by a combination of Leftists, pacifists, and Koreans affiliated with both the Soren and Mindan. In 1963, there were 23 such attacks, mainly against male secondary students, and perpetuated by right-wing student groups, *yakuza*, and assorted ruffians. One victim was beaten to death and two seriously injured. For the sake of perspective, though, it must be noted that the casualty rate on this and such occasions in South Korea under the then military regime was much larger with a higher death rate.

The Japanese authorities seem subsequently to have controlled violence relating to the Treaty. The next wave was, however, triggered soon afterwards by campaigns over the Foreigners' School Bills and the accreditation of the Korean University. There were seven cases of violence in 1966 and 15 in 1968. Next came the series of projected amendments to the Immigration Control Law, resulting in 20 attacks on Koreans in 1969, 34 in 1971, 33 in 1972, and 36 in 1973. Between these, there were 40 in 1970 relating to an attempt to resume the repatriation program to North Korea.

The assaults normally took the form of beating up a smaller group of Korean students—the primary target with their distinctive uniforms—by a larger group of Japanese students in public places such as the railway station. In Tokyo, these were frequently carried out by the ultra-right nationalist students of Kokushikan High School and University. This university, bearing a name in classical form denoting 'Hall of Patriots,' taught and trained students in militaristic style; the chancellor would preach in front of the students about the 'low intellect of the blacks, crudeness and cruelty of the whites, selfishness and greed of Chinese, inferiority of Koreans' and 'the Yamoto nation [an ancient and emotive name for Japan] who are the most superior in the world' (quoted in the magazine *Sekai,* August 1973). In the early 1970s, 15 April and 25 May, respectively Kim Il-sung's birthday and Soren's foundation day, were the days on which major assaults on Koreans were concentrated. During the first five months of 1973, 22 out of 26 incidents of violent assaults on Korean students were carried out by Kokushikan students. These were normally armed with a long umbrella but sometimes with a knife.

In a personal recollection by a Soren affiliate:

They make their gang attacks against students wearing the school pins of the Korean high schools. These right-wing Japanese youth would not, even by mistake, attack Koreans wearing the insignia of Japanese schools—the quiet, half-Japanese, who have 'assimilated well into our schools.' At a glance these latter are indistinguishable from the Japanese and above all they are not 'cheeky Reds.' The Korean students protest bitterly that it is the Japanese authorities, with their policy of forced assimilation, who have created the violence of the Japanese youth. (Pak Su-nam 1973)

More immediate influence came from the splinter Patriotic Party, which has contested elections unsuccessfully since the war. Its veteran leader, Akao Bin, was in earlier times so far to the right of Prime Minister General Tojo that, as a wartime Diet member, he was expelled from the sole legally permitted party for rebuking Tojo openly in the House.

Overall figures for later years appear to have been kept secret by the authorities. There was, however, no decrease in such cases. A series of disturbances arose in the mid-1970s from the kidnapping by South Korean agents of the leading opposition figure, Kim Dae-jung, in Japan, where he had taken refuge. This, of course, was generally resented as a violation of Japanese sovereignty. A group of lawyers and academics took action through the Supreme Court for the prosecution of those responsible, and the Japanese government was pressed to protest on Kim's behalf. In the event, he survived to contest elections after the democratization of South Korea in the late 1980s, unsuccessfully as it turned out.

A few years later came the Rangoon incident, when North Korean agents assassinated a number of visiting South Korean cabinet ministers at a time when the Japanese Red Army faction was implicated in or suspected of various involvements with North Korean as well as Arab terrorist plots. Next came the 1987 disappearance of a Korean Airlines aircraft over the Indian Ocean. This is said to have triggered the first attacks on Korean schoolgirls in Japan.

The aircraft in question, with 115 passengers aboard, had left Abu Dhabi for Seoul. Its last signals were received in the vicinity of Burma. Although no evidence on the incident was available for some time, the Japanese media immediately highlighted the statement of the KAL president that this was a 'terrorist act by Northern agents or the Red Army faction.' This was enough to set off a wave of attacks on Koreans as well as a long spell of police harassment on the pretext of investigating espionage or terrorist plots. Tensions were intensified in the concurrent lead-up to the Seoul Olympic Games, which the North and its sympathizers were thought intent on sabotaging. Possible North Korean participation in the Games had been ruled out after the KAL incident.

A joint Japan-South Korea summit conference drew up policies to combat sabotage, which were implemented on a large scale in Japan. The ruling LDP set up the Special Committee for Public Peace Measures, the Foreign Ministry its Red Army Liaison Measures Conference and the central Police Agency·its Olympic Security Measures Committee, International Terrorism Countermeasures Squad, and Guard Measures Committee. Prefectural Police Boards, beginning with Fukuoka in Kyushu, set up Seoul Olympic Security Measures Committees. Many Koreans were arrested, generally on formalistic charges of infringement of alien registration or radio regulations. These were regularly trumpeted in the press as spy arrests, though in virtually all cases those taken were quietly released when nothing substantial could be found. The main effect on the Korean community came from the sporadic violence directed at schoolgirls and even primary school pupils.

In 1989, the pattern was renewed with the accusations in the Diet that *pachinko* operators were financing the Socialist Party and supporting North Korea. Subsequent efforts at normalization of diplomatic relations with North Korea were interrupted by a new crisis arising from suspicions of that country's development of nuclear weapons. This in turn brought a spate of 158 reported attacks over the months April-July 1994. In the latter month, members of the Tokyo Lawyers Association presented to the United Nations Subcommission against Discrimination a report on over 100 cases of striking, kicking, and cutting hair and clothes. Some girls had their skirts cut open in the middle, one student had a liquor bottle thrown at her head by a drunkard, another was threatened with a knife, while another was spat at by a man who swore at her as a 'North Korean.'

In the Kyushu city of Oita, the International Relations Society raised money to replace torn Korean costumes in the nearby industrial city of North Kyushu. The press seems to have been less inflammatory than in Cold War times. A striking article by a professor at Soka University, established by a lay Buddhist movement with considerable Korean following, challenged the public to picture a situation where Japanese children abroad were being attacked, told to go back to Japan, or forbidden to speak Japanese, or to imagine American children in Japan being treated in this way.

In the disastrous Kobe earthquake of early 1995, the Korean and Burakumin quarter was severely affected. Total deaths were about 5,500 of whom 249 were foreign residents, presumably mostly Koreans. Another source counted 146 Korean dead. As the fires and disorder continued various expressions of apprehension showed that the experience of the 1923 Kanto earthquake had not been forgotten. The most dramatic incident occurred in the Diet itself at a session of the Upper House Budget Committee. In the course of a well-intentioned request for assurance that there would be no discrimination against Koreans in relief measures, a representative of the main opposition party mentioned that in a live telecast a Kobe Korean had expressed alarm at rumors that Koreans had started fires. Prime Minister Murayama assured him that there would be no discrimination but went on to express disapproval of the questioner's airing such a rumor, particularly as the session was being broadcast live. The Minister for Home Affairs also reprimanded him and demanded retraction of the remark.

The Soren, as ever, was quick to condemn the statement and to demand a retraction and apology, 'lodging a stern protest against this reckless remark, reminiscent of the ominous history of the massacre of Koreans at the time of the Great Kanto Earthquake.' The member expressed regret, though pleading for understanding that his intent had actually been to discourage such rumors. As it turned out, no violence arising from the earthquake was reported.

Part Four
CULTURAL ISSUES

14 Education

In recent years, something like 20,000 out of approximately 150,000 Korean children in Japan have been attending Soren schools. This is a decline from a peak of about 40,000 students a generation earlier. The decline is attributed partly to falling membership in the Soren (though some families with South Korean nationality also use the Soren system) and partly to a reduced birthrate.

The system comprises 1 university, 12 senior high schools, 56 junior high schools, 81 primary schools and 3 nursery schools. Attendance at full-time Mindan schools, in contrast, is less than 2,000 in four schools, each with all three levels. The course content of the Mindan schools is less ethnic in character than those run by the Soren.

Koreans chose Soren or Mindan schools to avoid the prejudice they encounter in Japanese schools, where nationality and ethnicity pose a problem in recognizing a student's individual success. One young girl commented:

> I received a phone call from one of my teachers. She called me to tell me that I was the top student in the Japanese high school and I was to be the valedictorian representing all the graduates for the graduation ceremony. The professors held a board meeting because I was a resident Korean. They concluded that, despite this fact, I should represent the students in the ceremony. (quoted by Yumi Lee)

However, students who complete the courses at Korean schools may find themselves at a disadvantage when they consider going on to a university or in preparation for career or work.

Soren schools

Let's look at how these schools are structured and supported. By 1990, the North Korean contribution to the Soren school system had dropped to about

10 percent of overall costs but the system remained viable on the basis of fees and donations, which increased with the growing affluence of the community. There has been some modest assistance for the Soren and the Mindan system from the local government in Osaka and the Yokohama area but no state aid. Textbooks are produced by the Soren's own publishers, though the editorial group regularly visits North Korea to consult experts there. Instruction has always been in Korean, though until recently limited to formal and literary modes, so that students have to fall back on Japanese to express intimate or everyday concerns. This division of linguistic labor has served to reinforce the Soren's institutional distinctiveness in the same way that many societies segregate the sacred from the secular, though among the latest generation a kind of Orwellian double-think seems to have developed.

The curriculum was standardized from 1963 and, although periodically revised, was, until a fundamental revision in 1993, completely dominated by a North Korean perspective, focused on the quasi-deification of the Great Leader, 'father Marshall' Kim Il-sung. Moral and civic education was based on semi-mythologized episodes from his life from childhood and the Revolutionary History associated with his son and heir apparent, the 'Dear Leader' Jong-Il. Discipline is generally based on self-criticism.

The 1993 curriculum revision marked a greater break with the past practice than any earlier development, reflecting the end of the Cold War and the predominance of a newer generation of teachers. There is less emphasis on the Kims (especially after Il-sung's death in 1994) and the personality cult was replaced with a more generalized patriotism, with less hostility directed towards Japan and South Korea (which is now ignored rather than attacked as an imperialist puppet). The use of Korean was broadened beyond the formal and public mode which was so closely identified with the previous order, though this in turn weakened the sense of segregation from the everyday milieu.

The North Korean context was replaced by that of life in Japan, as all thoughts of an ultimate return to Korea, even if unified, were fast vanishing. The study of Japanese history in Japanese was extended with a view to preparation for entrance examinations to Japanese senior high school or university. Beyond this, a more cosmopolitan context was introduced, including study of world religions and aspects of Western literature.

The Soren's success in setting up its ethnic education system and completing it by the establishment of an accredited university was the outcome of one of the most intense and protracted political confrontations in post-war Japanese history. Planning began soon after the Soren's establishment in 1955, and a start was made with a two-year college on the campus of an ethnic high school. When adequate finance was received from North Korea, a search was made for a suitable site. Attempts at purchase were, however, unsuccessful. So with the collaboration of the Japan-DPRK Society, a dummy company called the Kyoritsu Industrial Company was established and registered in the name of its Japanese members. This then obtained land in the Tokyo satellite city of Kodaira, built the necessary buildings, and leased them to Soren. Since ownership was Japanese, this arrangement avoided the risk of confiscation, which had been the fate of the Soren's predecessor, the Choren.

Courses began in 1959 and had the same content as those in North Korean universities. For some years there was no attempt to obtain Japanese accreditation, although this was desirable for such purposes as tax exemption and obtaining equipment on concession. Responsibility for accreditation lay with the prefectural authorities, at that time headed by Liberal Democratic Party governors who were not likely to favor ethnic education, though they did not interfere, since public funds were not involved. In 1965, the school applied for accreditation, but the governor withheld action, partly in response to pressure from the Education Ministry. Though the Ministry had no authority over accreditation, the Foreigner's School Bills proposed at the time would, if passed, have granted this authority, as well as power to close ethnic schools. The Ministry hoped soon to be able to exercise such power. The Korean University was, however, supported by unanimous resolutions in the Kodaira City and Tokyo Prefectural assemblies.

The situation took a favorable turn in April 1967 when the socialist governor Minobe Ryukichi was elected with combined Socialist and Communist Party support. This was part of a prevailing trend in the larger cities at that time, to some extent a reaction against the largely rural base of the LDP. For the next year, Minobe was besieged by the rival camps concerned with the accreditation question. Opposed to it were the LDP, extreme Right wing groups (who as usual threatened violence), and the Mindan, who, however, were uneasy with the racist tendencies of their 'allies.' Support came from a more cohesive alliance of academics, including university presidents, jurists, journalists, the largest trade union federation and, of course, the two Left-wing parties. Following proper procedure, Minobe referred the matter to his Private School Council. Their report was non-committal. Finally, however, in April 1968 Minobe felt strong enough to grant accreditation, with effective legal backing by an academic group headed by Yukura Ryokichi, professor of Administrative Law at Waseda University.

A unique description of the ambiance of the university is given by a researcher at the ANU, Sonia Ryang:

> For a visitor, it is necessary to produce a proof of appointment at the gate. The guard will normally double-check it by telephoning the person or department concerned. Once inside the premises, you will immediately perceive that you are in a different world. You will hear spontaneous singing; the songs are North Korean songs of revolution and devotion to the leadership. You will see female students wearing uniforms designed after Korean traditional costumes; it is compulsory to wear

them to attend lectures. You will smell Korean cuisine with generous use of garlic and chilies when walking by a large hall just beyond the front gate; the refectory caters for students and staff, as all the students without exception are accommodated on campus. Each dormitory has portraits of the two Kims. (Ryang 1996)

Some impressions of the Soren education system from the inside have been recorded by Pak Yang-ja. (Fukuoka 1991) Her father, a construction foreman, died when she was quite small, leaving an earnest wish for her to be educated at an ethnic school. Her mother moved to another town to be able to do this. Pak Yang-ja began at the school from primary school level and was forbidden to speak Japanese in school hours. She was generally happy except that the girls were all denied any alternative choice of club other than the Korean lute (*kayagum*) club, which did not much please her. While at primary school she still played with neighboring Japanese children, but this ceased soon afterwards.

She traveled to secondary school by train. She was not embarrassed by Japanese who stared at her Korean costume, feeling quite confident in her Korean identity. She had been taught how Korea in the Three Kingdom period (in the early centuries AD) had been more advanced than Japan and contributed much to its culture. She had been taught how the resistance movement under Kim Il-sung had fought for liberation from Japanese imperialism. She resented the Japanese for their ignorance of such matters.

She was encouraged to go on to the Korean University but hesitated because students had to board there and discipline was said to be severe. She also felt that the North Korean-style personality cult was unnatural and the level of indoctrination too intense. She conceded, however, that this was inevitable if a Korean identity was to be maintained in Japan. Once she became accustomed to life at the university, she came to feel that it was a refuge from family worries and other problems. On visits home, she argued bitterly with her mother, who had come to believe media reports on the evil of the Soren and North Korea. The mother wished she could break with the Soren, but all three of her children were deeply involved with it.

Pak Yang-ja tried a number of times to get a job during her first year at university but was unsuccessful because she was a Korean. Eventually, she obtained part-time work at a small bar. She had, however, to give this up after a week because the university did not allow first year students to work. During the short time she worked in the bar she was shocked at the frivolity of the Japanese students she worked with, who 'only talked about fashions and that sort of thing.' In her second year, a university teacher arranged for her to work part-time at a Korean restaurant.

Another young woman interviewed for *In Search of My True Self* described extracurricular study group contacts with Soren-affiliated students. She felt that this was a worthwhile experience but would not repeat it. If while they were discussing the issue of Korean reunification anyone expressed a deviant opinion, a senior member would announce 'I'll correct you there' and steer the discussion back to the approved line. When all were asked to describe frankly how reunification would affect them personally, she replied that if Korea were unified tonight she would take note of it in the next day's newspapers, but then carry on as usual. This was judged to be 'typical of those attending Japanese schools.' She felt uneasy at the conformity of the Soren students and says that, although she thinks of Korea as a special country, she does not feel it is her homeland.

Mindan schools

Then there are the Mindan schools. The amount of financial aid received from South Korea by the Mindan for educational purposes has been much less than that received from the North by the Soren, though apparently more per head for the much smaller number of students. Its programs are far less oriented towards identification with Korea. This is so partly because the Mindan tended to represent the more prosperous section of the Korean community, so that continued adaptation to the Japanese milieu remains an important concern. Its educational aim was to draw the line against complete assimilation, described as 'a betrayal of ethnicity and nothing other than self-rejection.' The Mindan's main effort is directed towards extracurricular ethnic classes in Korean language, history, and culture for Koreans in the public schools which most attend. Even in the few cases where the Mindan has operated schools, these have been accredited to teach the prescribed courses for Japanese public education, with the Korean element as subsidiary. Their main advantage lies in employing ethnic Korean staff, who impart some Korean orientation to their teaching. Korean names are, of course, also used.

The first aim of the Mindan program is defined as cultivating ethnic pride to counter the feelings of inferiority likely to be introduced by Japanese attitudes: 'The self-rejection involved in embracing this 'complex' and attempting to live disguised as Japanese is truly a blasphemy against humanity and personality. To use one's real name openly is the path to awakening as a Korean and self-affirmation.' (Min 1994)

The main areas of instruction are language, 'the soul of a people,' history to cultivate ethnic pride and particularly to counter the 'distortions' of Japanese representations of Korea, and Korean morals and customs, described as 'bringing education into real life.' Folk music and other arts are cultivated as the opportunity presents itself.

Adult education and part-time instruction are fairly widespread. These can include interested Japanese participants. Two centers of such education have received municipal support in the interests of improved understanding between Koreans and Japanese. They are the Trust and Love Academy in Yokohama and the Interaction Hall in nearby Kawasaki. These provide libraries and other resource materials for serious study, as well as a great variety of classes, ranging from language and historical studies to Korean cooking and folk arts.

In 1971, an umbrella organization intended to support Koreans in Japanese schools, as well as to promote understanding of Korea in Japanese education, was formed by teachers in Osaka. It was called Association for Research on the Education of Korean Children enrolled in Japanese Schools and produced supplementary texts, received a welcome from teachers in the field, and was extended in 1983 to the National Resident Korean Education Research Council. Its aims were:

> The education of resident Koreans will also contribute to the education of Japanese students in fostering a disposition to deepen friendship and solidarity with the Korean and other peoples of Asia and to promote peace between them. We will creatively develop educational and cultural activities with the aim of inculcating a correct understanding of Korea in the light of the historical relationship between Japan and Korea.

Developments of this kind began to gain considerable success in the late 1980s, largely stimulated by the Seoul Olympic Games, which first made South Korea a regular tourist destination. Before the Olympic Games, South Korean tourism was mainly Japanese 'sex tourism' (tour groups of Japanese men who visited Korea and other Asian countries solely to patronize prostitutes, strip shows, etc.) avidly promoted by the Park regime. South Korea's growing economic importance also helped to stimulate interest in the country and raised its status in Japanese eyes. This produced a different educational context from the earlier one which Yumi Lee had observed and deplored:

> Anything Korean has either been ignored or was made taboo throughout Japan. You notice it when trying to learn Korean. When I was a high school student, I studied Korean at Mindan. There was nothing out there for the study of Korean, no class, no textbook. Korean language was like something you learn underground. On the other hand, various textbooks for English and other languages were available in every bookshop. Most of the Japanese students chose French or German as their second foreign languages. It is a phenomenon: admiration of the West. They don't even think about the possibility of learning Asian languages. There are universities for foreign languages, which have various courses on European and Asian languages and even African ones. But no Korean. The only university I know with a Korean major is Osaka

Foreign Language University. There is no sign written in *Hangul*, even in the City Hall.

Regarding the last point, one mitigating factor is that, as literate Koreans would have a knowledge of Chinese characters, this would make it comparatively easy for them to gain a comprehension of Japanese notices, also mainly written in Chinese characters. Although usage differs, it does not present the sort of problem that a completely alien script would. In any case, long-term residents would be accustomed to using Japanese.

How language affects education

Although Korea has a considerable heritage of historical and literary works, until modern times this literature was entirely written in classical Chinese except for a body of popular fiction and songs composed in the vernacular in later centuries. This is comparable with the use of Latin in learned writing in Western Europe until the seventeenth century. It meant, however, that Japanese or others interested in traditional Korean literature would only need to read it in the original Chinese, without studying Korean as such. Written Chinese was always used in diplomatic relations. The *Hangul* phonetic script, devised in the fifteenth century, was described as 'teaching the people the correct sounds'—that is, it standardizing the pronunciation of Chinese characters. Otherwise, it was only used until modern times in informal writing. In an interesting contrast, the Chinese themselves never felt the need for a standardized pronunciation, and it has only been since the Communist regime introduced mass education that a popularized Mandarin has become standard in school education. By contrast, Japan has had an auxiliary phonetic script and voluminous indigenous literature since the eighth century. So the three languages present remarkably varied educational issues.

A 1993 survey shows quite widespread Korean language studies over 43 public and 73 private universities. The name used for 'Korean' shows marked divergence. Among the private universities in thirty-one cases, it is described as the language of Chosen (Choson in Korean) and in 26 cases as the language of Kankoku (Japanese rendering of Hanguk, or South Korea). Other institutions avoided the issue by describing the language as that of 'Koria,' from the European form derived from ancient Koryo, or as 'Hangul,' using the script to indicate the language. A couple use the term Chosen-Kankoku language, which seems more common among the state universities.

Early Korean-Japanese relations

This interest in language activity was paralleled by a wave of popular interest in early Korean-Japanese relations, as it affected the origins of the Japanese people and culture. Frequent media coverage of archaeological and anthropological studies helped stimulate this. The question of Japanese origins had long been taboo in polite society because the sense of Japanese uniqueness cultivated by modern nationalistic education made the idea of genetic links with other races unthinkable. In the pre-war State Shinto cult, the problem was evaded by the revival of ancient myths implying a special divine creation for Japan and its ruling house. This, however, was abolished after 1945. A vacuum was left, which only recently has been replaced by a growing curiosity about authentic antecedents.

Not surprisingly, this trend has been promoted by the Korean educational community. The significance of Korean relations with and contributions to early Japan has always been apparent, even from traditional sources. Recognition of this could improve both Korean morale and Japanese opinion of the Korean people. As a Mindan educator expressed it: 'We are a people of lofty pride in our high culture and long history which formed the fountainhead of Japanese culture.' (Onuma 1986) Another said: 'As the traces of the introduced culture can be discerned in this land of Japan where we live, a stratum is emerging particularly among our younger people who have what might be described as a sense of kinship with Japan and a certain type of confidence.' A girl quoted in *In Search of My True Self* relates how she felt better about being a Korean when a Japanese social studies teacher said: 'The Korean peninsula is Japan's mother. Japan grew by being suckled by its mother called Korea.'

Yumi Lee writes:

> Great contributions were made by those who came over to Japan in ancient times. They handed down Buddhist culture and formative arts. Knowledge of this contribution gives Koreans pride and confidence.
>
> Resident Koreans need an affirmative exposure to Korean culture to recover from self-rejection. This 'happy' approach to the issue is a must for our survival. While I was in America in 1991, I visited a teacher who conducts ethnic study classes for African-American and American Indian children. I reassured myself that self-esteem is the key. Resident Koreans can learn from these classes. In the Japanese education system, ethnic classes are not secure. It was striking in a TV interview to see a child showing his name written in *Hangul* and stating in a loud voice 'This is my name.'

From the Japanese side, the most striking literary source for Korea's role in Japan's origin is a compilation dated 815 AD of the genealogies of the nobility recognized at that time, entitled the *Newly Compiled Record of Titles and Clans*. Of the 1,182 clans listed, 326 are described as descended from immigrants of some centuries earlier, either Koreans of various stock or Chinese settled in Korea, much of northern Korea having been a Chinese province for some centuries around the early Christian era. The other clans are described as sons and daughters of deities who descended from heaven earlier and are divided among members of the Shinto pantheon whose shrines they served. Viewed historically, it seems that the 'immigrant' clans are those who arrived after the introduction of Chinese writing from Korea, so that their history could be recorded. Those who arrived earlier could not be the subject of record and therefore remained in the realm of mythology, or at best oral tradition. This, of course, is a universal phenomenon, as all races at the dawn of history date their origins either to some divine ancestry or to divine initiative, for example, God's call to Abraham.

Even such myths, however, hold useful clues to people's sense of their place in the world. The descent of the founding deities is described as occurring in two waves. The first arrived at the north coast of the Western projection of Honshu, opposite the southeastern coast of Korea, with a sizable island group between also figuring in myth. These first deities are described as so turbulent that the supreme deity, the Sun Goddess, later sent her own descendants to pacify them. These alighted in Kyushu, facing the south coast of Korea, with even more convenient island stepping stones between. The Sun Goddess's descendants, who became the Imperial House, are described as obtaining the submission of those already there and extending their conquests eastward against the indigenous inhabitants, a process taking many centuries. Their permanent headquarters were established in and behind Osaka.

The hypothesis of migrations from Korea underlying these myths has in general been well established by the excavation of tombs and ancient settlements in the two areas and in Korea itself. The study of the much more imposing tombs in and behind Osaka has been inhibited for various reasons. Whereas other remains of the age elsewhere in the world would be regarded as fit objects for archeological excavation, since no living person has any proprietary interest in them, the principal tombs here are attributed with some authenticity to historical emperors whose descendants still reign. They are therefore the responsibility of the Archives and Mausolea Division of the Imperial Household Agency, who are reluctant to allow any action that might amount to desecration. Another motive suggested by Korean interests is that Japanese authorities are afraid that archeology might expose a Korean origin for the Imperial House.

Something of the sort did happen in the early 1970s when a tomb, traditionally associated with the fully historical Emperor Mommu (697-708 AD) was accidentally disturbed by a typhoon. The burial chamber was found to be adorned by frescos depicting the Chinese sacred animals of the four directions and figures dressed in Korean costume of the time. Such cases were known in Kyushu but until then not so far east. One possible explanation lies in the circumstance that a generation before the Emperor's reign, two of the three states in the peninsula had been crushed by an alliance between China and a third, Silla. It appears that this event caused an exodus of elements of the ruling class to Japan, with which some had had close relations. Indeed, the Japanese had helped to defend one of the defeated states, its long-term ally, Paekche, in the southwest. The exodus could well have led to a new wave of Korean cultural influence in the Japanese court.

This remains a fragment in a potentially complex scene. A number of Chinese accounts of relations with Japan remain from the early centuries of the Christian era, while the Korean chronicles of the Three Kingdoms, though compiled in their present form considerably later, contribute a good deal. On the anthropological side, the Japanese language has its closest affinities with Korean and other languages of northeast Asia and indigenous beliefs, based on shamanism and animistic cults, have much in common.

Within this generally accepted framework, however, vigorous and long-running disputes have sparked between Korean scholars and their more nationalistic Japanese counterparts. Political considerations have played a crucial role in these. One of these issues centers on the Japanese belief, based on early chronicles, that from about the fourth to the sixth century, the Japanese court controlled a colony in the region of Korea nearest Japan called Kaya, where there was a group of six small states situated between Silla and Paekche. Japanese archeologists in the colonial period interpreted the similarity of remains there and in Kyushu as evidence of a Japanese influence, which was used to justify the Japanese presence in modern times. The Koreans, on the other hand, argue that this really means that Japan was settled from Kaya. A fifth century inscription in Chinese from the northern kingdom, Koguryo, mentions an incursion of the Wa, the then Chinese name for the Japanese, which the Japanese also once used to strengthen their case. But the Koreans argue that an expedition from Japan itself would not have been feasible and that these Wa were their kinsfolk in Kaya. Recent excavations in Kaya have revealed an impressive degree of civilization, which tends to favor the Korean view, but these discoveries have received good coverage in the Japanese media without any sign of negative reactions. The debate seems to be becoming more objective and less Japan-centered.

The other relevant theory has been the 'horse-rider' one. This implies that Japan was settled by nomads from further afield, who merely moved through Korea but need not be described as Korean. The importance of horses in the settlement of Japan is not in doubt, as tombs often contain bronze harness fittings, and at least one has a mural depicting a horse on a boat. A leading Japanese researcher in this field has used recent developments in genetics to argue that the mainland race with closest affinity to Japanese are the Buryat Mongols of Siberia. Present knowledge of the degree of development of the Korean states, however, makes it seem unlikely that nomads could have moved through them unimpeded in this period.

On the origins of the Koreans themselves, the ancestral legends of Koguryo and Silla are rather bizarre derivations from totemism, but the movement of the Paekche royal house from southern Manchuria is clearly established. It is in any case pointless to attempt to equate these fluid tribal societies with nation-states in the modern sense. On the other hand, the great contributions made by Paekche to Japan's cultural foundations has never been in doubt, as a variety of excellent artifacts received from or through it have been preserved, mainly in Buddhist monasteries down to the present day.

The improved treatment of this subject area in recent Japanese history textbooks seems likely to produce some effect on future Japanese attitudes of the kind.

15 Religion

Among the parallels to Anglo-Irish relations, Japanese colonization in Korea did not involve religious confrontations comparable with the level of conflict between Catholic and Protestant. The closest approach to this was the imposition of the artificial state Shinto cult, but, as in Japan itself, this was essentially a civic or patriotic duty, requiring participation in public rituals but not ruling out private commitment to other forms of religion. Tensions only occurred when these directly challenged the state cult, as in some Neo-Shinto and Neo-Buddhist movements in Japan and among some Christians in Korea, when severe repression occurred. Most people, however, kept the two spheres separate.

Since the abolition of State Shinto in 1945, religion has not involved any political or social tensions and as a result is not much raised in the considerable literature on the problems of the Korean community in Japan. It retains, however, some social importance as a component in the cultural heritage that the community tries to preserve.

Reasons for the lack of tension in this field stem in the broadest sense from the general east Asian tradition of approaching religion in a syncretic mode, rather than in the dogmatic or polemic mode traditional in the West and much of Islam. The general preference is for an eclectic synthesis of elements of varied origin, rather than stressing points of conflict.

A more specific reason is that the religious traditions of Korea and Japan are quite similar, enabling good mutual comprehension and occasional communion between them. The oldest of these are elements of shamanism, the primordial tradition of the whole of East and Central Asia, centered on shamans whose role is to communicate with the spirit world, mainly spirits of the dead or nature spirits. These shamans are usually women, called *mudang* or *simbang* in Korean and *miko* in Japanese Shinto. Women play an important part both in traditional cults and in related modern religious movements; this is also related to the Shinto belief in a female supreme deity.

In both countries, however, since the beginning of written records, functions of the kind more recognizable to Westerners as religious have been performed by Buddhism, with its voluminous scriptures, elaborate doctrines, and ritual and systematic ecclesiastical organization centered on the monasteries, as well as parish temples. In periods of greatest Buddhist influence, these were the mainspring of arts and culture of every kind, as well as serving social welfare functions. As in all other Buddhist countries, pre-existing beliefs were not suppressed but incorporated into one comprehensive cosmic scheme.

The other major tradition in both countries was Confucianism, which also cultivates reverential attitudes of a religious flavor, though in its dominant form of later centuries, known as Neo-Confucianism, it tended to minimize supernaturalism and concentrate on practical ethics. These are based on a conception of social hierarchies of a complementary nature, in which superiors set a good example to subordinates and safeguard their welfare, while subordinates loyally serve their superiors. Tyranny is condemned and certain notorious tyrants in Chinese history are used as a bad example. These social hierarchies are regarded as reflecting the hierarchies of nature based on the interactions of *yin* and *yang*. In society, the superior takes on the role of *yang* or Heaven and the subordinate the role of *yin* or Earth. Confucianism therefore traditionally functioned essentially as a cult of the state and family, with strongly patriarchal leanings.

Traditional religious observances drew on all these sources, with some additional elements from Chinese Taoism, another development from shamanism. In Korea, festivals still follow the Chinese calendar. Important occasions are the New Year, a general blessing and exorcism on the fifteenth of the first month, visits to graves on the first of the third month, the earth festival of the Zodiac Serpent on the third of the third month, the Buddha's birthday on the eighth of the fourth month, a form of the Chinese Dragon Boat Festival on the fifth of the fifth month, the Buddhist Ancestor Festival on the fifteenth of the seventh month, the Harvest Festival on the fifteenth of the eighth month, the Winter Solstice in the eleventh month, and the Year End closing the twelfth month. Confucian-type observances mark family occasions, as the state cult of course ended with the monarchy.

Christianity has made a big impact in Korea, beginning from the disturbed times towards the end of the monarchy. Under colonialism it flourished as a kind of alternative to Japanization, a role which the native traditions could not easily fill since they had so much in common with Japanese beliefs. Since liberation, Christianity has been promoted by United States influence and is divided roughly equally among Catholics, traditional Protestants, and American fundamentalists. The last contact produced a spectacular feedback to the United States itself in the Unified Family of the Reverend Sun Myung Moon, or the 'Moonies.' Figures for the adherents of Christianity in South Korea seem to come to between one-quarter and one-third of the population, though precise figures are open to doubt. For some, conversion to Christianity takes the participant halfway to secularism.

Yumi Lee, as a Christian, exemplifies this trend. Her preference for dating by the Christian era rather than by Japanese Emperors' reigns is symbolic of the thinking that led many to Christianity in the colonial era. About her religious beliefs, she writes:

> I was baptized right after I was born and there were times that I was saved by the Christian religion. God and Jesus Christ saved my maternal grandmother when she had to endure hardship. A number who devoted themselves to the resistance movement during the Japanese Imperialist era were Christians. Many were victimized in that era.
>
> My grandmother passed away on 5 November 1993. What would it have meant for her to live? I thought. She was born the year Japan invaded her country, got married young, then her husband was taken to Sakhalin for merciless labor from which he died. She took four children to Japan. Somehow she managed to survive. She was lonely but was strong and stout. Now she is in the hands of God.
>
> On 3 July 1994, relatives gathered and visited my grandmother's grave to bury her husband's ashes next to her. It was the first time in fifty-one years that my grandmother and her husband were united, in the grave, under the earth. My uncle and cousins went to Korea in the previous month and brought my grandfather's remains to Japan. Originally, his remains were taken by our uncle to Korea from Sakhalin, where he died. Now he is reunited with his wife fifty-one years after his death at the age of thirty.

Korean Christians in Japan would not have the same attachment as others to ancestral graves in Korea. Nor, of course, could Christianity in itself serve as a means of preserving Korean cultural identity. There seem to be some mainly Korean congregations, but otherwise they would associate with Japanese Christians, which was how Pak Sil met his Japanese wife. The contrasting case of an essentially Korean cultural continuity is illustrated by a 1994 account of a Korean Buddhist temple in Kodaira, where the Korean University is situated. It also indicates the general situation of the Buddhist community. (*The Japan Times* 24 August 1994)

The chief priest, Yun Pyo-gam, was born in Japan and had taught at the Korean University after graduating in engineering from Tokyo University. He decided to follow the example of his father, Yun Il-san, and uncle, Yun Il-yun, who had been Buddhist clerics. In Japan and to some extent in Korea, the parish clergy are not expected to be celibate. During the war, as part of the assimilationist program, Yun's father and uncle were both brought to Korea by the authorities to be trained in Japan. Their training was, however, carried out

148

under a senior Korean monk who had earlier been stationed in the Manjuji Temple in Kyoto, which mainly catered to Koreans.

After the War, Koreans remaining in Japan kept the ashes of the community's dead at such temples pending a possible return to Korea. Meanwhile, they held the services there, which would normally take place at the graves. As of 1994 there were 1,500 urns being held in the Manjuji. In 1965, the senior monk had moved to Kodaira, where he established the Kokuheiji Temple (in Korean Kukp'yongsa, meaning 'Temple of the Nation's Peace') to perform the same functions for Koreans in eastern and northern Japan. He was later succeeded by Yun's uncle and then by Yun himself. Meanwhile the temple in Kyoto had been left in the charge of Yun's father and then his brother Chon-an.

There were 1,300 urns held at the Kokuheiji, including the ashes of 300 who had died with no relative to mourn their passing. 'Some of them were found dead in their apartments, where they lived alone,' according to Yun. 'They were waiting in vain for the separated Koreas to be reunited after the war. Then they could return home.' No distinction is made here as to place of origin. Relatives at first would not consider burying the deceased in Japan, but 'such a long time has passed that the third and fourth generation Koreans have more or less given up the dream their ancestors cherished.' So the Kokuheiji finally became the first Korean temple in Japan to establish a Korean Buddhist cemetery, accessible to relatives who expect to remain permanently in Japan. Others, however, defer this action, maintaining that 'our ancestors hoped to see our countries reunited. They can't rest in peace until their wish is realized.'

There are about 200 such temples in Japan, most of them in the more Western areas of concentrated Korean population. Other references mention burials in Kyoto being conducted by the newer Koraiji (Japanese form of 'Temple of Koryo,' the name for united Korea), a branch of the Osaka temple Fugenji, affiliated with the Korean branch of the Zen or meditation school. The other main temple in Osaka, Tokokuji (in Korean T'ongguksa or 'Temple to Unify the Country') is strictly North-affiliated and serves the Soren, as well as acting as a channel of information from North Korea. Koreans living in areas without such services also hold funerals in Japanese Buddhist temples, while many of the temples catering for Koreans are themselves formally affiliated to a Japanese sect.

The type of institutions dedicated to shamanic practices are of a less regular and public character. In the early 1980s, Dr Helen Hardacre, then of the Berkeley Center for Korean studies, was able to closely observe these. She probably had a certain advantage in that these centers were largely operated by and for women. In Korea itself, feminists have favored the revival of the mudang cult as a native form of female culture capable of countering the masculine tendencies of the Confucian tradition. (Hardacre 1984)

The most characteristic of these temples—as they are called, though very different from the regular Buddhist type—are situated in mountain country easily accessible from population centers. In Japan, except for the Tokyo area, there are always mountains within easy distance. Hardacre found that there were about 42 temples accessible from Osaka, all exclusively serving the Korean community. About one-third are affiliated with Japanese Buddhist sects, especially of the Shingon or Mantra school, which sometimes licenses their officiants as lay ritualists, authorized to incorporate its rituals in temple observances. As is characteristic of all resident Korean life, the basic retention of a Korean identity is combined with elements of Japanese culture. Another peculiarity of these cults is the combination of shamanic and Buddhist elements in the same precinct and ritual sequence, in contrast to Korea where they are kept separate.

Structurally, these temples follow a general pattern. A modest residence is provided for the cleric in charge, with an altar used for ancestral rituals, an adjoining main hall, centered on a Buddhist image, either of the historical Buddha or one of the numerous other figures of Buddhist iconography, and a Star Chapel dedicated to Shamanic spirits. The Chapel is on higher ground and adjoins a natural waterfall (or one diverted from the nearby stream) which is used for lustration rituals.

The Star Chapel, the most characteristically Korean of these features, basically houses three scrolls. On the principal one, a central Buddha figure is surmounted by seven figures in the forms of Buddhist saints, representing the stars of the Dipper (as it is also called in East Asian terminology) which revolve around the Pole Star, measuring time, seasons, and human destiny. Around and below are attendants, most dressed in Confucian scholar attire, together with the Taoistic philosopher Lao Tzu and four minor Buddhist figures. This main scroll is flanked by two others, one depicting the Mountain God with attendant tiger and the Sea God with attendant dragons. These figures are in Confucian style. Although these designs are peculiarly Korean, the scrolls in most cases have been produced by Japanese temple artists in Osaka, following Korean prescriptions.

The ritual calendar partly follows the Korean pattern sketched above. Retained are the events of the fifteenth of the first month, the Serpent Festival, the fifth of the fifth month, and the Winter Solstice. The Buddha's birthday and the Ancestor Festival are common to both countries, but the Koreans maintain the Chinese calendar while the Japanese usually follow the Western one. The other main events are adopted from Japanese practice. One, on the fifteenth of the second month, is dedicated to the popular Japanese set of Seven Gods of Fortune, of whom one is Shinto, three of Indian origin, one Chinese Buddhist, and two Taoist. The sixth of the sixth month and the ninth of the ninth month are dedicated to the 'Eight Hundred Myriad Deities,' a Shinto theme designed to cover all nature.

The most essentially shamanic rituals are held at any time requested by parishioners, whenever they feel the need to dispel misfortune, which may involve the healing of illnesses, or to promote good fortune. A typical ritual begins with a female shaman, here called a *simbang,* going into a trance with the aid of bells, music, and sometimes a hypnotic dance. She is then possessed by spirits which deliver oracles in Korean. These spirits are usually ancestral but are sometimes nature spirits or Buddhist guardian deities. As most parishioners understand little of this, the message has to be interpreted into Japanese for them. It usually involves some information or instructions regarding the problem at hand. A Buddhist ritual follows, conducted either by a visiting monk or more often by a male or female *posal* or lay ritualist. This consists of the creation and conveying of merit to the spirits by reciting Buddhist scriptures in the Chinese version pronounced Korean style, supplemented by Sanskrit mantras transliterated in *Hangul*—altogether a remarkable cultural composite.

Similar services are available in the city, where the *simbang* maintains a small chapel at her residence and usually visits parishioners as required. Visits are also made by mountain temple clerics to city dwellers in need of help.

Hardacre observed another type of religious occasion when she joined a group of Korean women accompanying a party of mixed Japanese and Korean pilgrims to a sacred mountain further inland. The women followed the Japanese rituals precisely, including a strenuous ascent into a sacred cave. At night, however, left to themselves, the Korean women relaxed

> in the friendly intercourse their culture prizes, and female Japanese pretenders to gentility abhor: loud, contentious conversation, omission of honorific language, sitting cross-legged, cheerfully trading insults, and so on. At dinner they consumed considerable quantities of beer and sake and engaged in vigorous dancing, ribald singing, and charades in a style of only slightly restrained eroticism, some dancers clad only in underwear.

After a short sleep, however, small groups of women took turns visiting a chapel of the Eight Naga (Buddhist dragon) Kings, where a *posal* received the spirit of the Nagas and delivered messages to her companions.

A more modern mode of involvement of Koreans with Japanese Buddhism has been participation in the Soka Gakkai ('Value Creation Association'), by far the most successful of the lay religious movements or 'new religions' which have been a marked feature of modern Japanese society. It has been the only one to found a successful political party, the Komeito or Clean Government Party. During the period of Liberal Democratic Party dominance it became the second largest opposition party, and was a member of the governing coalitions during the two short-lived succeeding Cabinets. Koreans have been active in the party, too. The main attraction to them has been the movement's universalistic attitude, which has also led to its success overseas. Involvement in such a movement would, however, do little to preserve Korean cultural distinctiveness.

Kim Il-myon disparages this development:

> In my opinion the beginning of assimilationist tendencies among certain Koreans goes back to their becoming adherents of the new religion Soka Gakkai which spread like an epidemic in the midst of the Korean War. At that time the whirlwind of aggressive proselytizing by the Soka Gakkai was much talked about throughout Japan. It was described as kidnapping the people of the lower strata in Japanese society. This included many resident Koreans. These had been regarded as having a strong ethnic consciousness but after the outbreak of that war a rather large number fell away. Without any clear prospect of repatriation, they assumed that Japan would become their semi-permanent abode and shut themselves up in their own burrows. At that time the Soka Gakkai made house-to-house visits to the neglected Korean ghetto in Asakusa and arranged residence registration for its inhabitants. People were startled that it was taking over the role that should properly belong to political reformists in the Communist or Socialist parties. The ghetto's people doubtless surrendered to the 'Buddhist faith' of the Soka Gakkai because of its unexpected sympathy and kindness. (Kim Il-Myon 1978)

Though not intended to be favorable, these comments recognize the Soka Gakkai's advantage in being able to provide an emotional appeal which Left-wing parties could not, particularly since the Soka Gakkai could relate to elements in Koreans' cultural background.

16 Apartheid in death: The Korean atomic bomb memorial

The wartime Korean population of Hiroshima consisted partly of pre-war immigrants and partly of wartime conscript laborers. The latter were fairly numerous, as Hiroshima was a military command and industrial center of some importance, though not of high enough strategic priority to be attacked earlier. Figures for Korean victims, as for the overall total, are rather indefinite, as they include both those killed immediately from the blast and firestorm and those dying later from radiation sickness, many within the first weeks while radioactivity in the area remained dangerous, and others suffering from delayed effects over some decades. Among the total of more than 300,000 covered in the complete records of the Atomic Bomb Casualty Commission, Koreans are difficult to identify because of the enforced use of Japanese names. Other sources indicate that at least 50,000 would have been exposed to the attack. Of these, it appears that 20,000 to 30,000 would have died in the days and months following the attack.

Koreans suffered disproportionately because their dwellings were concentrated in the central industrial zone and because, unlike surviving Japanese who could take refuge with their ancestral families in the countryside, they had little recourse other than to remain in the radioactive area in what shelter they could improvise from the ruins. They were also accorded the lowest priority in the limited treatment or relief available. In the words of a later memoir:

> The army treatment center in the school was full of people. Some had already died there. There was a mountain of dead people, bloody, and without eyes. Some were still breathing. A military doctor was treating the burns with oil and when it was my turn he asked, 'Where were you hurt?' When I answered 'I was in Kamiyacho' he shouted at me, 'You, you're a Korean, aren't you?' and glared at me as though he wanted to kill me. I thought, 'Am I going to get help from a scoundrel like this?' and I left just as I was. (Pak Su-nam 1973)

The Peace Memorial Park at the epicenter, at a fork between two rivers, gradually took shape in the years after the peace treaty and a cenotaph was dedicated to all the victims, but nothing marked the disproportionate number of Koreans involved because names were all in Japanese form. In 1970, the Mindan obtained approval to erect a separate memorial at a site across one of the adjacent rivers. Although outside the Peace Park, it had a particular link with the Korean community, as it was the site of the discovery of the body of Prince Yi Gu, the most socially distinguished of the Korean victims. He was a nephew of the last Korean king who had consented to the treaty of annexation and was given high rank in the Japanese peerage, together with others in the royal house. Prince Yi Gu had been a Lieutenant-Colonel in the Japanese Army and his insignia had attracted attention among the mass of corpses in the river.

The memorial consists of an inscribed granite column supported by the statue of a symbolic mythical tortoise. The central inscription, in Chinese characters equally intelligible to Japanese and Koreans, reads: 'Memorial for Korean Atomic Bomb Victims,' using the South Korean term for Korea. Beside it, in ceremonial seal characters, is another reading: 'In memory of Prince Yi Gu and the other 20,000 or more Souls.' Below is a horizontal engraving in English: 'The Monument in Memory of the Korean Victims of the A-Bomb.' On the left side of the pillar is engraved the South Korean flag, though this is also the flag that was in use before annexation. Its use is defended on the grounds that it can be taken in a broader sense as symbolizing the restoration of Korean traditional culture. On the back of the memorial is a Korean description in *Hangul* of Korea's experience of Japanese colonialism. An adjoining plaque explains the background of the memorial's construction in Korean, Japanese, and English. The whole is surrounded by plantings of hibiscus, Korea's national tree, and stones brought from Korea.

As with all other matters affecting the Korean community, the memorial has been a focus of constant controversy. Soren affiliates could not accept it as representing all Koreans, as the flag, even in its pre-annexation aspect, was associated with the discredited monarchy, also represented here by the mention of Prince Yi Gu. They could not accept the argument that the Prince's inclusion symbolized a rehabilitation or reconciliation for collaborators, and from 1975, they began agitating with the city administration for a memorial of their own, which was resisted as being too inflammatory. A wider movement for the memorial's relocation to the Peace Park was began by the poet Oh Tokai, backed by a Japanese sympathizer in the interests of all-round reconciliation. Oh disassociated himself from both North and South as the champion of an autonomous Japan-resident community, symbolizing his stand by pronouncing his name in the Sino-Japanese style. The city replied that regulations banned any new construction in the Park, that any memorial considered must be all-inclusive to avoid conflict, and that the existing cenotaph in any case embraced all.

The situation changed in 1990 when President Roh visited Japan. Roh asked the Japanese government to furnish all available information on the wartime labor draft and to compensate Korean atomic bomb victims, many of whom had returned to Korea and needed assistance. The government agreed to form a foundation for this purpose, with funds to amount to ¥4 billion over some years.

The Hiroshima city administration responded to these moves by offering to erect a non-controversial monument in the Peace Park by the next municipal Peace Memorial Ceremony on 6 August and named a committee to arrange this. The committee recommended a neutral inscription to read 'Memorial for Atomic Bomb Victims,' identifying Korea only by a Korean classical expression to the effect that their precious deaths would remain fragrant forever in people's hearts, with two *Hangul* symbols reading 'tribute to the dead.' But although leading members of both Mindan and Soren supported the plan, it was frustrated by protests from various quarters and the only immediate outcome was the introduction for the first time of special mention of Korean victims, beginning from that year's Memorial Ceremony.

It is ironic that for years the Koreans fought against discrimination in death and demanded that they take their rightful place on the official Peace Memorial to the victims of Hiroshima. However, when Japanese authorities agreed to their inclusion, the Koreans realized that this would mean not only the end of their difference as Koreans but also the loss of a physical site deeply identified with Korea and Koreans. By remaining outside the park, it provides a constant reminder of Korean alienation and thus a site for continued struggle. In this case, to win the battle would be to lose the powerful symbol of Korean heritage.

Whether in life or in death, the Koreans face the same dilemma. Naturally they demand an end to discrimination and to be treated as equals to the Japanese. But in the Japanese milieu this can only be achieved, if at all, at the cost of total assimilation, which means a loss of identity and personal history.

17 Korean writers in Japanese

In spite of the obstacles facing Koreans resident in Japan, a number of Koreans have made a considerable impact in the literary field, and several have won prestigious literary prizes. This owes something to the general Japanese background where, since early in the century, a prodigious literary output has been the product of high popular literacy and feverish social development. Within this context, moreover, Korean writers have had the advantage that the literary world has generally been less conformist and more cosmopolitan than the ruling establishment. This means that Koreans and others of varied background have had a better chance of their work being judged on its merits. Here I will introduce a few representative figures.

Yumi Lee mentions one who struck a chord with her:

> Yi Yang-ji, a second generation Korean woman, wrote a novel called Yuhi, a story about a third generation woman of that name who went to Korea to study and find herself, and ended up coming back to Japan. There must be many young resident Koreans who empathized with her. I was one of them. The author won the well-known Akutagawa Prize.

This is a top-level literary prize, named for Japan's premier master of the short story. The heroine of the novel, modeled on the author herself, enrolls at a top-class South Korean university to major in language studies. Although she acquires some skill in writing Korean, she never achieves fluency in speech. Even in her writing, as a Korean character notes, she alternates some very effective passages with others that sound like literal translations from the Japanese. So she abandons her course, returns to Japan and from then on writes only in Japanese, which the author herself did very successfully.

As a Japanese critic notes, Yuhi is caught not only between Japan and Korea but is also cut off from plebeian Korean life by her middle-class upbringing. While in Korea, she enjoys listening to the traditional flute but blocks her

156

ears against the popular songs played on buses. She is not much impressed by South Korean literature but is charmed by the pre-war pro-Japanese writer Yi Kwang-su. She admires the fifteenth century king who created the *Hangul* script but is repelled by its exclusive use among the masses. Presumably she misses the effectiveness and associations of Chinese characters. Her story conveys well the internal complexities experienced by an individual Korean.

Yi Kwang-su is described as the father of modern Korean literature and as 'Korea's Tolstoy.' He belonged to the early generation of upperclass students who came to Japan before full annexation, initially in the hope that their studies could contribute to the progress of Korean society. He eventually developed an assimilationist posture. His first piece was published in a Japanese university magazine in 1909, when he was seventeen. He became an established writer during the World War I and in the late 1930s participated in a Korean Writer's Association, writing on themes supporting Japan's war effort. In Yi Yang-ji's novel, the protagonist has to be discreet about her partiality for Yi Kwang-su in post-war Korea.

Yi Yang-ji is a writer who is described as belonging to a generation beyond the period when Japan-resident Korean writers had a choice between assimilationism and reversion to an autonomous Korean identity. The prototypes of these two trends are respectively Chang Hyok-ju and Kim Sa-ryang. Chang became the most prominent Korean writer in the pre-war period and early opted for Japanese as a world language which would reach a wider audience than Korean. He made his debut, however, in the radical 'proletarian literature' movement which enjoyed a vogue in Japan for a few years around 1930, before more reactionary trends became dominant.

His initial orientation arose from his early experience as a schoolteacher in rural Korea, where he was moved by the hardships of the peasants and by a widespread student movement of 1929 protesting against discrimination in schools. Chang's first published piece appeared in an anarchist magazine in Japan in 1930. In 1932, he won a prize awarded by the liberal magazine Kaizo (Reconstruction) for the novel *Hungry Ghosts,* which was hailed as revealing to the world for the first time the existence of a Korean writer.

He returned to Korea for a time and wrote about landless peasants forced to emigrate to Japan or Manchuria. The colonial administration in Korea banned his writing on this theme. He decided that his future as a writer could lie only in Japan. There, however, the proletarian literature movement was in rapid decline, through both suppression and disillusionment, so he joined earlier contacts and established a new magazine Bungei *Shuto* (Literary Metropolis) which ran successfully until after World War II. Chang wrote for it until 1938, re-oriented towards psychological themes of the kind that have formed the mainstream of 'pure literature' in Japan. One example is the story of a struggle between two men over a prostitute in a Korean village. He treated this purely as a psychological study without reference to the social dimension that had been his earlier concern. Such works were well received in Japan.

Chang was still living mainly in his native place, Taegu. In 1935, he published some pieces in Korean, but these were poorly received in local vernacular literary circles. He attributed this reaction to jealousy and left Korea for good, though he continued to write about Koreans in the Japanese setting. He married a Japanese woman and from 1939 adopted a pro-establishment line. In an 'Open Letter to Korean Intellectuals,' he argued that assimilation would cure the characteristic Korean faults of 'impulsiveness, poor sense of fairness, jealousy, and perversity.' He also wrote several pieces about the late sixteenth century Japanese invasion of Korea, presenting the Japanese side in a favorable light which coincided with the line of contemporary expansionism. He did not join Yi Kwang-su's Korean Writer's Association, though their line was similar, because he regarded himself as a 'Japanese writer born on the peninsula.' Instead, he joined the Japanese Writers' National Service Association.

As well as writing, he made propaganda visits to Korean communities in Japan, Manchuria, and China but seems to have foreseen Japan's defeat in good time and returned before the surrender. He retained his standing in literary circles and on the occasion of the Peace Treaty was naturalized as Noguchi Minoru, using his wife's surname. He settled in the vicinity of an ancient shrine known to have been founded by Korean settlers many centuries ago and continued writing into the 1980s.

A writer who took the opposite approach and advocated a reversion to an autonomous Korean identity, Kim Sa-ryang, was about ten years younger than Chang. When he began writing in 1939, he had to adjust from the outset to the dominant reactionary trend in society and culture. This was the year when the imposition of Japanese names began in Korea, followed by a ban on Korean language newspapers, and the arrest of members of the Korean Language Society. Chang introduced Kim to the magazine *Literary Metropolis*, which soon published his first piece. This dealt with the theme of a mixed Japanese-Korean youth beginning, as often, by despising his Korean heritage but in the end finding some pride in it. The treatment, however, was kept well within the then current official line of 'Japan and Korea indissoluble,' with Koreans as supposedly equal partners with Japan and in theory deserving respect as such.

Paradoxically, considering the suppression of Korean culture, a 'Korea boom' in Japanese literary circles manifested itself in special issues featuring Korean writers in magazines and anthologies of Korean writing. All this was, of course, in Japanese, but included translations from Korean originals. Kim Sa-ryang published several translations from works in Korean by Yi Kwang-su. This led him in a second successful piece, *Temba* (Pegasus) to criticize Chang's line that composition in Japanese was essential to a wide readership. This piece is a satire on writers attempting to capitalize on political trends and argues that those more at home in Korean should compose in it, if necessary for translation, rather than be constricted by a medium that will lose the essential viewpoint they wish to convey.

Over the next few years Kim mainly wrote stories set in the last years of the Korean kingdom, partly aimed at dispelling nostalgia for the 'good old days' of a society that was, in fact, hopelessly decadent. This could be construed as justifying the Japanese takeover but is actually meant to suggest an image of a future, revived Korea that would be free of the faults of traditional late Korean society. In 1944, he gave up writing, unable to pursue the themes he wished. For a time, he worked in a technical school. The following March, while visiting Beijing, he escaped to the Communist headquarters in Yenan and joined the free Korea alliance led by Kim Tu-bong. When World War II ended he moved to North Korea and died in action with its army in the Korean War.

Koreans writing in Japanese up to the mid-1960s tended to be dominated by concern or nostalgia for Korea, partly because those born in Korea were still in the majority and partly because a possible return to Korea could still be considered. Representative of this phase is Kim Sok-bom whose best known works relate to the uprising on Cheju Island which began in April 1948 and continued as a guerrilla campaign for eight years, overlapping the whole of the Korean War. Kim had been born in Japan but, like the majority of the Osaka community, was descended from Cheju people. He made a visit to the island and was able to obtain much first-hand material which he incorporated into vivid psychological treatments of the uprising.

This uprising began to smolder in protest against the United States Occupation policy of retaining former pro-Japanese collaborators in the administration. The United States forces believed these collaborators to be reliably anti-Communist. Preparations to set up the United States' nominee Syngman Rhee as the head of a South Korean government, splitting the peninsula, was the spark that ignited the fire of protest. Protests arose elsewhere but were more easily suppressed than on Cheju, where the islanders' solidarity was exceptional. The uprising was ultimately crushed by means that were virtually genocidal.

This theme was also taken up by other writers. Kim's literary philosophy, however, aimed at attaining a 'universality through creativity,' transcending local peculiarities such as those separating Japanese and Korean modes of expression. This orientation grew stronger as the Korean community grew away from Korea and was exposed to ever-widening influences.

Characteristic of the next phase was Kim Hak-yong who tended to react against Korean ethnocentrism, which he identified with his tyrannical father. The theme of the tyrannical father is a common one in portrayals of Korean family life in Japan, though in Kim's case there is some recognition that injuries inflicted on himself and his mother were indirectly caused by Japanese society, through the hardships visited on the two preceding generations. His

159

highly introspective writing is described as exceptional in capturing the Korean community's psychology.

Kim suffered from a stammer. He turned this to good account in a piece 'Frozen Mouth,' for which he won the Literature Prize in 1966. He describes his writing as a process of breaking through a series of shells, each piece representing a past self. In this particular piece, the central character seeks to define his real self as something independent of his identity as a stammerer, finding himself most fully in wordless sexual union.

He portrays marriage as 'not a scene of tranquillity but something oppressively mysterious, as hard to define as grasping a slippery seaslug.' In scenes of domestic discord, the narrator finds himself shouting at his wife in exactly the same tones as his grandfather and father had in their time. Kim's effort to distance himself from his father eventually took a political turn. When his father sided with the North, he came to side with the South and to restrict his negative images of Korea to the North only. He became a columnist for the Mindan-affiliated *Toitsu Nippo* (Unification Daily). He wrote his last piece of fiction in 1978 and from then on confined himself to politically oriented articles. But his process of 'breaking shells' had come to an end, and he took his own life in 1985. Although suicide has been extremely common among Japanese writers, Kim's case is exceptional among Koreans. Professor Kim Yang-gi, in his psychological study, has pointed out that Koreans as a whole see no positive meaning in suicide.

The first Korean to be awarded the Akutagawa Prize was Yi Hoe-song, who was born in Japanese Sakhalin in 1935. His father had a high status in the mines there as he held office in the Kyowakai (the organization to control Koreans). He was also a tyrannical father and husband. Yi's mother died young, so he had little exposure to Korean and 'inevitably' enjoyed mastery of Japanese only. Nevertheless, he believed that his 'life consciousness' imparted a distinctively Korean quality to his writing, by which he aimed to achieve a 'Korean literature in Japanese.' He was concerned that younger generations of Koreans in Japan should not find in this mere exoticism.

He was awarded the Akutagawa Prize in 1972 for a piece described as a 'requiem for his dead mother.' In general, however, his writing was concerned with social or political themes, such as his major work *The Unfulfilled Dream* (1979) which suggests that a true Korean can only hope to establish an identity through 'the democratization of South Korea and the unification of the fatherland.' From the mid-1980s, he managed a magazine and wrote some plays. In 1994, he was awarded the Noma Literature Prize for a semi-historical work, *Travelers Through the Century.*

He traveled widely, twice visiting his grandparents, who had remained in Sakhalin. In the United States, he met Nym Wales, the first wife of Edgar Snow and a writer on both the Korean and Chinese revolutions. Visiting Yunnan in 1937, she interviewed the Korean leader, whom she called Kim San,

160

and published his life-story in *Song of Ariran* (named for a national folk song). Yi also visited the Korean community in Central Asia as well as Koreans in Europe. After one visit to South Korea, he was refused further entry because his attitude to the North seemed too favorable, though he appears to have attempted to be impartial.

A writer of about the same vintage, praised by a leading Japanese critic for his 'minute observation and lucid expression' was Kim Tae-saeng. In addition to his natural gifts, he experienced extraordinary vicissitudes which covered a wide gamut of the more tragic aspects of Korean life in Japan. This provided material for highly representative and moving literary expression.

He was born on Cheju Island in 1924. His father abandoned the boy and his mother and left to seek his fortune in Japan. When Kim Tae-saeng was aged five, his mother was obliged to remarry and leave him, as is customary, to the care of his father's relatives. These sent him to Osaka, where an uncle and an aunt took care of him. He never returned to Cheju. His remarkably vivid, if idealized, memories of this island merged with those of his lost mother as a generalized image of a lost Korea. This in turn merged with nostalgia for a lost language, as Japanese naturally took over. He thinks of Japanese as a 'foster-language' merging with the image of his aunt, who was his foster-mother.

His aunt seems to have looked after him well but died of tuberculosis when he was about 13. He did his utmost to relieve her final sufferings and may have been infected himself at this stage, though acute symptoms only appeared much later. His uncle was of little help, being of the callous and drunken type so often produced by the harsh environment. At some stage, he advised the boy to seek out his father in Kyoto, and Kim spent some time with him from the late 1930s. This experience was also a bitter one, since his father was often in trouble with the police and spent much of the money the boy was able to earn. In one episode, the boy bought a camera, hoping to become a photographer but had to sell it for ¥30 to pay for medical treatment. When the police, in the course of their frequent arbitrary investigations of Koreans, found the money—a sizable amount—in his possession, they held him on suspicion of theft. When he was cleared they returned the money to the father, who spent it on himself.

Kim was back in Osaka during most of the war and soon after the surrender heard that his father had died. On inquiring through the Kyoto police, he was struck by the large number of Korean names on their books—Japanese in form, of course, but clearly adapted from Korean names. At a prison hospital, he was given his father's ashes in a small pine box. He wrapped the ashes in a handkerchief and discarded the box as a symbol of the Imperial system. He avoided Kyoto for many years because of its bitter associations.

He enrolled in a course in dairy farming with the idea that he might take up such work in Cheju but went down with tuberculosis and spent seven years in a sanitarium, where he reflected on the equality of Japanese and Koreans in the face of death. On being discharged in 1955, he felt that he had been 'reincarnated.' Having meanwhile had the leisure to become interested in literature, he offered a piece to the magazine *New Korea,* edited by Kim Tal-su, another leading figure in the early post-war literary scene. It was published under the title 'The Phlegm Glass.' It was based on his aunt's last days, illuminated by his own later experience. This was the beginning of his lifelong mission to commemorate this earlier generation, saving them from the 'second death of oblivion.'

He then became active on the editorial committee of *Literary Metropolis,* regularly publishing narrative pieces and reviews. From 1958, he took up the theme of the Cheju uprising but gave more emphasis to the psychology and ideals of the rebels, rather than the horrors of the conflict itself. From 1962 to 1970, he wrote little, since his time was taken up with editing the pro-North periodical *Toitsu Hyoron* (*Unification Review*). From 1972 until his death in 1986, he produced a stream of fine pieces beginning with 'Ashes,' an account of his experiences with his father. He also began a vogue of writing about life in Ikaino, the epicenter of the Korean community in Osaka. In some cases, this took the form of 'internal exoticism.' Kim developed some optimism about the 'self-purifying power' of Japanese society, which he hoped might produce a 'Japan not for Japanese only.' For most Koreans, the image of the lost homeland remains in the background, over the sea.

Kim expressed this last sentiment in a vivid epigrammatic haiku. It refers to the custom of drying seafood on the beach in the sun:

> The cuttlefish's eyes are moist
> As it dries, facing the sea.

A woman writer who has recently achieved some prominence is Chong Chu-wol, poet, essayist, and short story writer. She is second generation, knowing only Japanese, as she grew up and lived in the provincial town of Saga in western Kyushu until she graduated from junior high school. At that time, she moved to Osaka in the hope of finding wider options. Though not distinguishable as Korean, she was generally mocked for her dialect, which is strikingly different from either Kansai or standard Japanese. Driven to spells of embarrassed retreat in the privy, she began to compose defiant verses of 'urine and feces.' Her first employment, slapping heels onto plastic sandals, later inspired evocative writing about girls high on glue singing to each other. She married a resident Korean who is described as 'attractive,' but a happy marriage did not solve the problem of the instability of a life where social advancement was blocked. She eventually ran a bar to support her family, which included three children and a sister-in-law.

The context of Chong's writing is also located in the 'exotic' Ikaino quarter and continues to center on the local women—in sweatshops, hawking mar-

162

ginal goods on street quarters, or collecting scrap metal, and trying to make enough money to employ the service of shamans. Chong's style, however, is more picturesque than might be expected from such humble, even tragic, material. One critic has noted that 'puns, aggressively obscure Chinese characters, and neologisms run rampant as an act of vengeance for entrapment in the colonizers' language.' (Field 1993). She also holds firm to Korean ethnicity, hoping that the shared experience of both North and South oriented Koreans in Japan may ultimately contribute to the homelands' unification. She remains 'undaunted by the contempt that Koreans in the homeland feel for overseas compatriots.'

18 Conclusion

The Korean community in Japan is deeply divided: politically, economically, socially, and culturally. One aspect of the cultural division is the degree of assimilation into Japanese society. It is difficult to say much about the highly assimilated groups because these are not the sort of people who speak out, write books and pamphlets, join activist groups, demand rights, or are anxious to be interviewed. Neither Yumi Lee nor anyone else can speak for the whole Korean community. During the final stages of writing this book, I was fortunate in being able to read the manuscript of Sonia Ryang's book on the North Korean community in Japan. Yumi Lee's information and the better part of the published material deals mainly with the Southern rather than Northern perspective. Thanks largely to the efforts of both Ryang and Lee, we now know vastly more and have a more balanced picture of the whole Korean community in Japan. However, in the assimilation spectrum from Korean to Japanese, both Ryang and Lee, in their own different ways, are acutely aware of their Koreanness and are unlikely candidates for assimilation.

Perhaps Yumi Lee's parents are in some ways more typical Korean Japanese. Although discriminated against in her youth, Yumi Lee's mother harbors no ill feelings towards the Japanese and is cool towards her daughter's activism on behalf of the Korean community. Towards the Japanese she is thankful for small mercies. Remembering her youth, including the hardships suffered from discrimination, she remembers the Japanese neighbors 'who were kind to us. They gave us food and lent us money without any guarantee that the loans would be returned. I was then genuinely happy.' From her more central position in the Korean community, Yumi Lee's mother put her finger on the sort of problem overlooked by the activists.

My mother says that it is more unbearable to be discriminated against by Koreans than by Japanese. In Korea we are looked down upon because we live in Japan. Discrimination also exists among Koreans depending on one's place of origin in Korea. The Korean community itself has created discrimination within a discriminatory society.

But Korean sins hardly excuse the Japanese, who as the party with all the real power have a lot to answer for. The colonial origins of the Korean community in Japan, far from giving the Japanese an additional reason to despise the Koreans, should give them the responsibility to atone for the sins of the past. The way the Koreans were first colonized and then stripped of their Japanese nationality should be recognized by the Japanese instead of forgotten.

However, great legal and even social gains have been made by the Korean community over the last few decades. The heroic struggles of the Korean activists led the way, but their efforts would have been in vain had it not been for the independent though tardy Japanese legal system. Nevertheless, Koreans are still subject to discrimination in important areas such as housing, marriage, and employment. Japan emerges from this story as a racist society badly in need of positive anti-discrimination legislation and a changing consciousness of the rights of minority peoples.

In those few areas, such as in writing, entertainment, and services, where the Koreans do not suffer discrimination, they have done well. The remarkable achievements of Korean writers in Japanese hint at the tremendous cost to Japan of discrimination. Discrimination in Japan, as anywhere in the world, stifles talent, destroys creativity, and causes suffering. For Japan to prove that it has entered the modern world socially and culturally as well as economically, it will be necessary publicly to recognize that massive discrimination against Koreans, Burakumin, and other minorities exists. The current policy of sweeping all under the carpet and consigning racist history to a memory hole (at least for foreign consumption) deludes no one.

A symbolic but meaningful improvement would be made if the Korean community in Japan were described as Korean Japanese. Only when the Koreans are accepted as Japanese, as a special type of Japanese, will the path be cleared for a resolution of this problem. For the Japanese to demand total assimilation is just as unrealistic as the Southeast Asian governments who demand instant and complete assimilation of their own Chinese minorities. It is only natural for a minority to cling to its cultural identity especially when it is despised and under pressure. Both the Koreans and Japanese are uncomfortable with 'Western' ideas of pluralism, but is there any other solution?

Admittedly, there is a long way to go. The Chinese American who is both Chinese and American at the same time is almost incomprehensible in the Japanese milieu. Nevertheless, the overwhelming majority of the Korean community in Japan, excluding only those at the opposite poles of the assimilation spectrum, are not accepted by either the Koreans in Korea as genuine Koreans or by the Japanese as Japanese. They are neither, but share characteristics of both. Having lived in Japan for generations, they should surely be described, at least in English and preferably in Korean and Japanese, as Korean Japanese.

Select Annotated Bibliography

The basic sources used in this book are noted in this bibliography. In cases where substantial amounts have been quoted, attribution is made in the text. Many of these sources are pamphlets or special interest publications, and therefore circulated only in a limited way and not widely accessible. Several were obtained through Yumi Lee and Kawashima Megumi. The more important studies are briefly annotated.

Arai Masahiro 1992. Nit-Cho Yuko eno Michi (The Path to Japanese-Korean Friendship). Self-published, Kyoto. A critical study of the earliest and modern relations between Japan and Korea.

Asahi Shimbunsha (ed) 1992. Iutsaram: Rinjin—Utoro Kikitori (Iutsaram: Neighbors—Interviews on Utoro). Gikai Janaru (Assembly Journal) Company, Kobe. Collected material on the Utoro mass eviction case.

Bridges, Brian 1993. Japan and Korea in the 1990s. Edward Elgar Publishing Company, Aldershot UK.

Buraku Kaiho Kenkyusho (Buraku Liberation Research Institute) 1993. Human Rights in Japan from the Perspective of the International Covenant on Civil and Political Rights: Counter Report to the Third Japanese Government Report. Osaka. Covers Burakumin, Koreans, Ainu, foreign workers, women, and disabled persons.

De Vos, George A. 1993. Social Cohesion and Alienation: Minorities in the United States and Japan. Westview Press, Boulder USA.

Field, Norma 1993. 'Beyond, Envy, Boredom and Suffering: Towards an Emancipatory Politics for Resident Koreans and Other Japanese,' Positions: East Asian Cultures Critique 1:3, Duke University Press, 640-70.

Fukuoka Yasunori et al. 1991. Honto no Watakushi o motomete (In Search of my True Self). Shinkansha, Tokyo. Interviews with young resident Korean women on their life stories.

Hardacre, Helen 1984. The Religion of Japan's Korean Minority: The Preservation of Ethnic Identity. University of California, Berkeley.

Hayashi, Koji 1991. Zai-Nichi Chosenjin Nihongo Bungaku Ron (Literature in Japanese by Koreans Resident in Japan). Shinkansha, Tokyo.

Horumon Bunka Henshu Iinkai (Editorial Committee for Korean Community Culture) 1991. Horumon Bunka 1 (Korean Community Culture, Issue 1), Shinkansha, Tokyo. First in an occasionally published miscellany of pieces on community life. 'Horumon' is the name for Korean organ meat barbecue, here used as a popular symbol for the community.

_____ 1992. Horumon Bunka 3, Shinkansha, Tokyo.

Inoue, Hideo and Chong Cho-myo 1993. Kankoku-Chosen o shiru tame no 55 sho (55 chapters for learning about Korea). Akashi Shoten, Tokyo. Introductory material on all aspects of national life and history.

Kanagawa-ken Shogaibu Kokusai Koryuka (International Interaction Section, Kanagawa Prefecture Public Relations Office) 1992. Hamgge: Tomoni (Hamgge: Together) 1992. Akashi Shoten, Tokyo. A miscellany of popular writing and information from the local Korean community.

Kang Chae-un et al. 1989. Zai-Nichi Kankoku-Chosenjin: Rekishi to Tembo (Koreans resident in Japan: History and Prospects). Rodo Keizaisha (Labor Economics Company), Tokyo.

Kang Ch'ol 1994. Zai-Nichi Chosenjin no Jinken to Nihon no Horitsu (Human Rights of Koreans resident in Japan and Japanese Law).Yusankaku, Tokyo.

Kim Il-myon 1978. Chosenjin ga naze 'Nihonmei o nanoru noka?' Minzoku Ishiki to Sabetsu (Why do Koreans use 'Japanese Names?' Ethnic Consciousness and Discrimination), San'ichi Shobo, Tokyo. A comprehensive coverage of related issues, illustrated by vividly told case histories.

Kim Myong-shik 1987. Shimon Kyohi no Shiso (Principles of fingerprint refusal). Akashi Shoten, Tokyo.

Kim Yang-gi 1993. Nomen no yona Nihonjin (Japanese compared to Noh Masks). Chuo Koronsha, Tokyo. A searching, objective and lively contrastive study of Japanese and Korean psychological traits.

Kyoto-shi Kokusai Koryu Kyokai (Kyoto City International Interaction Society) 1994. Zai-Nichi Kankoku-Chosenjin wa ima: sono Seikatsu to Iken (Japan-resident Koreans Today: their Life and Views). Kyoto. A series of symposia with participation by Yumi Lee.

Lee, Changsoo and De Vos, George A. 1981. Koreans in Japan: Ethnic Conflict and Accommodation. University of California, Berkeley. A collection of 15 articles on history and major issues.

Lee, Yumi 1995. Unpublished memoirs.

Lee, Yumi 1991. Who has heard Japanese-born Koreans' Voice? Friends World College, Kyoto. A booklet prepared for her American speaking tour in 1991.

Min Kwan-shik (trans. Kim Kyong-duk et al.) 1994. Zai-Nichi Kankokujin no Genjo to Mirai (Present conditions and future of Korean residents in Japan). Hakuteisha, Tokyo. A translation and up-dating of a thorough, statistically based academic study written in South Korea.

Minzokumei o torimodosu Kai (Association to recover Ethnic names) 1990. Minzokumei o torimodoshita Nihonseki Chosenjin (Koreans of Japanese nationality who have recovered their ethnic names). Akashi Shoten, Tokyo.

Minzoku Sabetsu to tatakau Renraku Kyogikai (Mintoren: Liaison Association for fighting Ethnic Discrimination) 1989. Zai-Nichi Kankoku-Chosenjin no Hosho Jinkenho (Compensation and Human Rights Law for Koreans residents in Japan). Shinkansha, Tokyo. Proposed draft legislation to cover all aspects.

Mitchell, Richard H. 1967. The Korean Minority in Japan. University of California Press, Berkeley.

Miyata Setsuko, Kim Yong-dal et al. 1992. Soshi Kaimei (Creation of Surnames and Changing Given Names). Akashi Shoten, Tokyo. A thorough study of the imposition of Japanese names in colonial Korea.

O Kyu-sang 1992. Zai-Nichi Chosenjin Kigyo Katsudo Keisei Shi (History of the Formation of Entrepreneurial Activities by Koreans resident in Japan). Yusankaku, Tokyo. A thorough, statistically based account of North Korea affiliated business activities.

Oblas, Peter B. 1995. Perspectives on Race and Culture in Japanese Society. The Edwin Mellen Press, Lewiston, New York. Media coverage on recent studies of Japanese origins.

Onuma Yasuaki and Suh Yong-dal (eds) 1986. Zai-Nichi Kankoku-Chosenjin to Jinken (Koreans resident in Japan and Human Rights). Yuhikaku, Tokyo. A series of symposia on major issues.

Pak Sunam 1973. Mo hitotsu no Hiroshima: Chosenjin-Kankokujin Hibakusha no Shogen (Another Hiroshima: Testimony of Korean Bomb Survivors). Sanseido, Tokyo (English translation forthcoming).

Research/Action Institute for Koreans in Japan 1990. Japan's Subtle Apartheid. Tokyo. Articles by activists on key topics.

Ryang, Sonia 1997. North Koreans in Japan: Language, Ideology, Identity. Westview Press, Boulder USA.

Shimada Haruo 1994. Japan's Guest Workers: Issues and Public Policies. University of Tokyo Press, Tokyo. A study of the problem of legal and illegal foreign workers.

Tanaka Hiroshi 1991. Zai-Nichi Gaikokujin (Aliens in Japan). Iwanami, Tokyo. A lucid, compact treatment of all foreign groups in Japan by a leading figure associated with Mintoren who assists foreign students.

Teiju Gaikokujin to Kazokuho Kenkyukai (Association for Research on Permanent Resident Aliens and Family Law) 1991. Teiju Gaikokujin o meguru

Horitsu-jo no Kadai (Legal Issues regarding Permanent Resident Aliens). Nihon Kajo Shuppan KK (Japan Loose-leaf Publishing Company), Tokyo.

Tokoi Shigeru (ed) 1990. Ima Zai-Nichi Chosenjin no Jinken wa (Human Rights of Korean Residents in Japan). Nihon Hyoronsha (Japan Review Company), Tokyo. Articles by specialists with text of relevant laws.

Weiner, Michael 1994. Race and Migration in Imperial Japan. Routledge, London.

Yamada Terumi and Pak Chong-myong (eds) 1991. Zai-Nichi Chosenjin (Koreans resident in Japan). Akashi Shoten, Tokyo. Articles contributing little-known data on Korean issues.

Yoneyama, Lisa 1995. 'Memory Matters: Hiroshima's Atom Bomb Memorial and the Politics of Ethnicity,' Public Culture, 7:499-527, University of Chicago.

Yoshida Seiji 1983. Watakushi no Senso Hanzai: Chosenjin Kyosei Renko (My War Crimes: The Forced Draft of Koreans). San'ichi Shobo, Tokyo.

Glossary of Japanese and Korean terms

Buraku(min) (Japanese): Ghetto (dwellers, outcasts)
Chima-chogori (Korean): Two-piece female costume
Hangul (Korean): Phonetic script
Kana (Japanese): Phonetic script
Kayagum (Korean): Native lute
Kempeitei (Japanese): Military-political police
Kimchi (Korean): Chili and garlic pickled cabbage
Kyopo (Korean): Overseas Korean
Miai (Japanese): Date with a view of possible marriage
Miko (Japanese): Shamanic medium or ritualist (female)
Mudang (Korean): Shamanic medium [not much ritualist function]
Okonomiyaki (Japanese): Pizza-like cooking
Pachinko (Japanese): Pinball
Posal (Korean): Buddhist lay ritualist
Shiromuku (Japanese): White wedding robe
Shochu (Japanese): Grain or potato spirit
Simbang (Korean): Shamanic medium
Yakuza (Japanese): Professional gangster
Yangban (Korean): Premodern scholar official class
Yin-yang (Chinese): Negative and positive poles of nature
Zai-nichi (Japanese): Acronym for 'Japan-resident'